Synchronicity Unveiled

Exploring the Interplay of Chance and Meaning

Peter Kattan

Petra Books
www.PetraBooks.com

Synchronicity Unveiled
Exploring the Interplay of Chance and Meaning

ISBN - 979-8-8691-9564-7

Preface

Welcome to the exploration of synchronicity, where the seemingly random intersections of events in our lives are unveiled as threads woven into the fabric of existence. In these pages, we embark on a journey through the enigmatic realms of psychology, physics, spirituality, and philosophy to unravel the mystery of synchronicity.

As we delve into the heart of this phenomenon, we begin with an inquiry into its nature, pondering the elusive connections that defy conventional explanation. From Jungian theory to the intricacies of quantum mechanics, we seek to define synchronicity and understand its profound implications.

Drawing from historical perspectives and everyday encounters, we uncover the origins of coincidence and contemplate its significance in shaping our perceptions of reality. Through the lens of psychology, we explore the depths of the collective unconscious and the archetypal patterns that underlie synchronistic experiences.

Venturing into the realm of quantum physics, we peer into the intricacies of the quantum field, where entanglement and connectivity blur the boundaries of space and time. Through the exploration of statistics, symbolism, and intuition, we endeavor to decipher the hidden meanings behind synchronistic events.

From dreams to serendipitous encounters, from scientific discoveries to spiritual insights, we traverse diverse landscapes of thought and experience, seeking to grasp the essence of synchronicity in all its manifestations.

But as we journey deeper into the labyrinth of synchronicity, we confront its shadow side—the unsettling realm of negative experiences and existential uncertainties. Yet, even in the midst of chaos and doubt, we discover a profound sense of order and purpose that transcends rational understanding.

In our quest for meaning, we contemplate the timeless mysteries of existence, contemplating the interplay of chance and destiny, chaos and order, in the synchronistic dance of the universe.

Ultimately, we come to realize that synchronicity is not merely a phenomenon to be observed, but a profound invitation to embrace the interconnectedness of all things and to awaken to the infinite possibilities that lie beyond the veil of everyday reality.

So join us now, as we embark on a journey of exploration and discovery, navigating the twists and turns of synchronicity's labyrinth, and embracing the mystery that lies at its heart.

A major part of this book was written with the help of artificial intelligence, specifically using ChatGPT 3.5.

Best regards,

Peter Kattan   May 2024

Contents

Introduction: The Mystery of Synchronicity

The phenomenon of synchronicity has long intrigued and baffled humanity, challenging our understanding of causality and the nature of reality itself. Coined by the renowned Swiss psychiatrist Carl Gustav Jung, synchronicity refers to meaningful coincidences that seemingly defy conventional explanations. These occurrences carry a sense of significance or resonance, often manifesting as uncanny parallels or serendipitous encounters. While skeptics may dismiss synchronicity as mere chance or wishful thinking, its mysterious nature continues to captivate the human imagination and inspire philosophical inquiry.

Jung introduced the concept of synchronicity in the 1950s, drawing from his studies in psychology, philosophy, and Eastern mysticism. He proposed that synchronistic events arise from the interconnectedness of the collective unconscious, where archetypal patterns and universal symbols intersect with individual lives. Jung's fascination with synchronicity stemmed from his own personal experiences, as well as his observations of patients' dreams, fantasies, and synchronistic encounters during therapy sessions.

Unlike traditional cause-and-effect relationships, synchronicity operates beyond the confines of linear time and rational explanation. It suggests a deeper, acausal principle at work in the universe, where meaningful connections can occur spontaneously across vast distances of time and space. Examples of synchronistic experiences abound in various cultures and contexts, ranging from dreams and visions to encounters with strangers, symbolic coincidences, and intuitive insights.

Dreams, in particular, often serve as conduits for synchronistic messages and symbols. Many individuals report experiencing dreams that seem to foreshadow future events, offer guidance, or provide insights into their innermost thoughts and emotions. These synchronistic dreams often coincide with significant life transitions or moments of personal transformation, serving as symbolic mirrors of the psyche.

Encounters with strangers or chance meetings with acquaintances can carry profound synchronistic significance. These serendipitous connections may lead to unexpected opportunities, collaborations, or friendships that resonate deeply with one's inner journey. Such encounters highlight the interconnectedness of all beings and the mysterious ways in which the universe orchestrates meaningful connections.

Symbolic coincidences also play a central role in synchronicity, with certain symbols or motifs recurring across different contexts and cultures. These synchronistic symbols often carry archetypal meanings that resonate with the collective unconscious, serving as signposts along the journey of self-discovery and spiritual awakening. Whether encountered in dreams, everyday life, or cultural artifacts, these symbols invite contemplation and interpretation, offering insights into the deeper patterns of existence.

Intuitive insights and gut feelings represent another dimension of synchronicity, guiding individuals along their path with flashes of inspiration or inner knowing. Trusting in these intuitive nudges can lead to synchronistic encounters or serendipitous outcomes that defy logical explanation. By cultivating awareness and attunement to these subtle signals, individuals can navigate life's twists and turns with greater clarity and purpose.

The implications of synchronicity extend far beyond the realm of personal experience, raising profound questions about the nature of reality, consciousness, and the interconnectedness of all things. While skeptics may dismiss synchronicity as mere coincidence or subjective interpretation, its mysterious nature challenges us to reconsider our assumptions about the fabric of reality.

At its core, synchronicity suggests a universe imbued with meaning and purpose, where every moment is pregnant with possibility and significance. By embracing the mystery of synchronicity, we open ourselves to the magic and wonder of existence, recognizing that the threads of destiny are woven through the tapestry of our lives in ways that transcend our understanding.

The mystery of synchronicity invites us to explore the hidden connections that unite us with the cosmos, reminding us that we are part of something greater than ourselves. As we navigate the currents of life, may we remain open to the synchronistic signs and symbols that guide us on our journey of self-discovery and awakening. In the dance of synchronicity, we find glimpses of the divine orchestration that shapes our destinies and binds us together in a web of meaningful relationships.

Chapter 1 - Defining Synchronicity: From Jungian Theory to Quantum Connections

Defining synchronicity is akin to grasping at smoke - elusive, yet undeniably present. Coined by the eminent Swiss psychiatrist Carl Gustav Jung, synchronicity represents a departure from traditional cause-and-effect relationships, delving into the realm of meaningful coincidences that seem to defy rational explanation. Jung introduced this concept in the 1950s, drawing from his studies in psychology, philosophy, and Eastern mysticism.

At its core, synchronicity suggests a deeper order or intelligence at work in the universe, where seemingly unrelated events are connected by a hidden thread of meaning. Unlike mere chance occurrences, synchronistic events carry a sense of significance or resonance, often manifesting as uncanny parallels or serendipitous encounters. Jung proposed that these meaningful coincidences arise from the interconnectedness of the collective unconscious, where archetypal patterns and universal symbols intersect with individual lives.

To understand synchronicity, it's essential to distinguish it from mere coincidence. While coincidences are random and devoid of inherent meaning, synchronicity involves a meaningful correlation between inner and outer events. For instance, a person may have a dream about a long-lost friend and then receive an unexpected phone call from that friend the following day. While skeptics may attribute such occurrences to chance, proponents of synchronicity argue that there is a deeper, acausal connection at play.

Jung's concept of synchronicity has been met with both fascination and skepticism within the scientific community.

Critics argue that synchronicity lacks empirical evidence and falls outside the purview of traditional scientific inquiry. Jung himself acknowledged the limitations of empirical validation in the realm of synchronicity, noting that it operates beyond the confines of conventional causality.

In recent years, advances in quantum physics have offered intriguing parallels to Jung's concept of synchronicity. Quantum theory challenges our classical notions of space, time, and causality, suggesting a nonlocal and interconnected nature of reality. Some physicists have proposed that quantum entanglement, where particles become correlated in such a way that the state of one instantly influences the state of another, may offer a potential mechanism for synchronicity.

Furthermore, the emergence of quantum consciousness theories posits that consciousness plays a fundamental role in shaping reality. According to these theories, the observer's consciousness collapses the wave function, determining the outcome of quantum events. This intimate connection between consciousness and the quantum realm echoes Jung's notion of synchronicity, where inner states of mind are reflected in outer events.

In light of these developments, the bridge between Jungian psychology and quantum physics becomes increasingly apparent. Both frameworks challenge the Newtonian paradigm of a clockwork universe governed by deterministic laws, instead pointing to a reality imbued with uncertainty, interconnectedness, and the potential for meaningful coincidences.

While the mystery of synchronicity may never be fully explained by science, its implications for our understanding of consciousness, reality, and the human experience are profound. By embracing the enigma of synchronicity, we open ourselves to the possibility of a universe teeming with hidden connections and hidden meaning. Whether viewed through the lens of psychology, philosophy, or quantum physics, synchronicity invites us to explore the deeper mysteries of existence and our place within the cosmic tapestry.

Synchronicity, as defined by Carl Jung, is a concept that challenges traditional notions of causality and randomness. It suggests that meaningful coincidences exist beyond mere chance, pointing to a deeper order or intelligence at work in the universe. Jung proposed that these synchronistic events arise from the interconnectedness of the collective unconscious, where archetypal patterns and universal symbols intersect with individual lives.

While skeptics may dismiss synchronicity as pseudoscience, Jung himself acknowledged its elusive nature and the limitations of empirical validation. Nevertheless, recent advances in quantum physics offer intriguing parallels to Jung's concept, suggesting a nonlocal and interconnected nature of reality. Quantum entanglement and quantum consciousness theories propose mechanisms that resonate with the idea of synchronicity, where inner states of mind influence outer events.

The convergence of Jungian psychology and quantum physics challenges conventional paradigms, offering a new perspective on the mysteries of existence. Rather than viewing the universe as a deterministic machine, synchronicity invites us to contemplate a reality filled with hidden connections and meaning. It transcends disciplinary boundaries, inviting exploration from psychology, philosophy, and physics alike.

Synchronicity remains a profound enigma that defies easy explanation. Whether regarded as a psychological phenomenon, a philosophical concept, or a quantum mystery, it prompts us to reconsider our understanding of consciousness and the nature of reality. As we delve deeper into the mysteries of synchronicity, we may uncover profound insights into the interconnectedness of all things and our place within the cosmic tapestry of existence.

Synchronicity, with its elusive nature, continues to intrigue scholars and thinkers across disciplines. Despite the skepticism it faces in scientific circles, the concept persists as a lens through which to explore the mysteries of existence. Jung's insights into synchronicity have spurred diverse interpretations and applications, ranging from depth psychology to spirituality and beyond.

One avenue of exploration lies in the realm of spirituality and mysticism. Many spiritual traditions embrace the idea of synchronicity, seeing it as evidence of a higher intelligence or divine plan at work in the universe. From the concept of karma in Hinduism and Buddhism to the notion of providence in Judeo-Christian thought, synchronicity resonates with the belief in a meaningful and interconnected cosmos.

Synchronicity finds resonance in the realm of creativity and inspiration. Artists, writers, and musicians often describe experiences of synchronicity fueling their creative process. They speak of moments when ideas seem to flow effortlessly, when unexpected connections emerge, and when the boundaries between self and other dissolve. In such moments, synchronicity becomes a source of inspiration and guidance, leading individuals to new insights and expressions.

Furthermore, the practical implications of synchronicity extend into everyday life. Many people report experiencing synchronistic events that guide them in decision-making or offer reassurance during challenging times. Whether it's a chance encounter that leads to a new opportunity or a series of coincidences that point the way forward, synchronicity can serve as a source of comfort and guidance in navigating life's uncertainties.

In the realm of therapy and self-discovery, synchronicity plays a significant role in Jungian analysis. Therapists often explore clients' experiences of synchronicity as a means of uncovering unconscious patterns and facilitating personal growth. By paying attention to synchronistic events, individuals can gain insight into their inner world and develop a deeper understanding of themselves and their relationships.

Synchronicity remains a rich and multifaceted concept that defies easy categorization. Whether viewed through a psychological, spiritual, or creative lens, it invites us to reconsider our assumptions about the nature of reality and the interconnectedness of all things. While skeptics may dismiss it as mere coincidence, those who embrace synchronicity see it as a profound reminder of the mysteries that lie beyond our understanding. As we continue to explore and ponder its implications, synchronicity continues to offer new avenues of inquiry and discovery, inviting us to explore the depths of the human experience and the universe itself.

Exploring synchronicity reveals a tapestry of interconnectedness that transcends conventional boundaries. Beyond its psychological and spiritual dimensions, synchronicity intersects with broader philosophical inquiries into the nature of reality and consciousness. Philosophers throughout history have grappled with questions of causality, randomness, and meaning, finding in synchronicity a provocative challenge to prevailing worldviews.

One aspect of synchronicity that resonates with philosophical inquiry is its implications for free will and determinism. Traditional notions of causality imply a linear progression of events governed by deterministic laws, where each cause leads inevitably to its effect. Synchronicity disrupts this linear model, suggesting that meaningful coincidences can occur independently of conventional causal relationships. This raises profound questions about the nature of agency and the extent to which individuals can shape their own destinies.

Furthermore, synchronicity prompts reflection on the nature of reality itself. In a universe where synchronistic events occur, reality appears to be far more complex and interconnected than our everyday experience suggests. This challenges our perception of reality as static and objective, inviting us to consider alternative frameworks that account for the dynamic interplay of inner and outer phenomena.

The study of synchronicity intersects with inquiries into the nature of time and space. Traditional notions of time as a linear progression from past to future are called into question by synchronicity, which suggests a more fluid and nonlinear conception of time. Synchronistic events challenge our understanding of space as a fixed, separate entity, pointing instead to a reality where boundaries blur and connections abound.

In the quest to understand synchronicity, philosophers draw on diverse intellectual traditions, from Eastern mysticism to existentialism and beyond. Each tradition offers its own perspective on the nature of reality and the human condition, shedding light on different facets of the synchronicity phenomenon.

The exploration of synchronicity opens up new avenues of philosophical inquiry, challenging us to rethink our assumptions about the nature of reality, consciousness, and the human experience. As we grapple with the mysteries of synchronicity, we are reminded of the profound interconnectedness of all things and the limitless possibilities that lie beyond our current understanding. In this sense, synchronicity serves not only as a subject of philosophical inquiry but also as a catalyst for philosophical exploration, inviting us to venture into the depths of existence in search of deeper truths.

Delving deeper into the philosophical implications of synchronicity unveils a rich tapestry of inquiry that extends beyond conventional boundaries. One avenue of exploration lies in the realm of metaphysics, where synchronicity challenges prevailing notions of causality and determinism. Metaphysical inquiries into the nature of reality often grapple with questions of ultimate causation and the interconnectedness of all things, finding in synchronicity a compelling example of the intricate web of existence.

The study of synchronicity intersects with epistemological concerns about the limits of human knowledge and understanding. Synchronistic events defy easy explanation within the confines of traditional rationality, prompting reflection on the nature of knowledge itself. How do we come to know the world around us, and what role do intuition, insight, and subjective experience play in our understanding of reality? These are questions that synchronicity forces us to confront, challenging us to expand our epistemological horizons beyond the confines of empirical observation and logical deduction.

Furthermore, the exploration of synchronicity raises ontological questions about the nature of being and existence. What is the ultimate nature of reality, and how do synchronistic events fit into our conceptual framework of the cosmos? Some philosophers posit that synchronicity points to a deeper underlying unity that transcends the apparent multiplicity of phenomena, suggesting that reality may be far more interconnected and interdependent than we commonly perceive.

Besides to its metaphysical and epistemological implications, synchronicity also has ethical and existential dimensions. The recognition of meaningful coincidences in our lives can lead to a profound sense of interconnectedness and purpose, prompting us to reevaluate our relationships with ourselves, others, and the world around us. Synchronicity invites us to reflect on questions of meaning, purpose, and morality, challenging us to live in alignment with the deeper patterns and rhythms of existence.

Exploring synchronicity from a philosophical standpoint delves into the depths of existential inquiry, prompting reflection on the fundamental nature of human existence. One avenue of philosophical exploration lies in the realm of phenomenology, which seeks to understand the structures of subjective experience. Synchronistic events, with their uncanny ability to evoke a sense of significance and resonance, challenge phenomenological theories of perception and consciousness, inviting us to reconsider the relationship between the subjective and objective dimensions of reality.

The study of synchronicity intersects with existentialist concerns about the nature of freedom, authenticity, and the search for meaning in a seemingly indifferent universe. Existential philosophers such as Jean-Paul Sartre and Martin

Heidegger grappled with questions of individual agency and responsibility in the face of an inherently ambiguous and absurd world. Synchronicity adds another layer of complexity to these inquiries, suggesting that even in the midst of uncertainty and randomness, there may be hidden patterns and connections that imbue life with meaning and purpose.

Furthermore, the exploration of synchronicity raises questions about the nature of time and temporality. Traditional conceptions of time as a linear progression from past to future are called into question by synchronistic events, which seem to transcend conventional notions of causality and sequence. This prompts philosophical reflections on the nature of temporality, causation, and the relationship between the present moment and the unfolding of events.

Besides to its existential and phenomenological dimensions, synchronicity also has implications for ethics and moral philosophy. The recognition of meaningful coincidences in our lives can lead to a heightened sense of interconnectedness and empathy, prompting ethical reflection on our relationships with others and the world around us. Synchronicity invites us to consider questions of moral responsibility, compassion, and the interconnectedness of all living beings in the web of existence.

The study of synchronicity from a philosophical perspective opens up new horizons of inquiry, inviting us to explore the nature of consciousness, time, freedom, and ethics in light of the mysterious interplay of meaningful coincidences. As we grapple with the philosophical implications of synchronicity, we are reminded of the profound mysteries that lie at the heart of human existence, and the infinite possibilities that unfold when we open ourselves to the interconnectedness of all things. In this sense, synchronicity serves not only as a subject of philosophical speculation but also as a catalyst for deeper insights into the nature of reality and our place within it.

The philosophical exploration of synchronicity leads us to consider its implications within the realm of ontology - the study of being and existence. Synchronicity challenges conventional ontological frameworks by suggesting that reality may be far more complex and interconnected than we perceive. This raises questions about the nature of existence itself: What does it mean for events to be connected in meaningful ways that transcend traditional causal explanations? How do we conceptualize the fundamental nature of reality in light of synchronistic experiences?

Furthermore, the study of synchronicity intersects with the philosophy of mind, which seeks to understand the nature of consciousness and subjective experience. Synchronistic events often involve a deep resonance or sense of significance that seems to arise from within the individual's psyche. This prompts philosophical inquiries into the relationship between the mind and the external world, and the role of consciousness in shaping our perception of reality. Does the mind play an active role in creating synchronistic experiences, or do they arise independently of individual consciousness?

Chapter 2 - The Origins of Coincidence: Historical Perspectives

Coincidence, that curious dance of chance and circumstance, has fascinated humanity since time immemorial. From ancient civilizations to modern societies, humans have grappled with the notion of seemingly random events aligning in unexpected ways. While the concept of coincidence may appear straightforward, its origins and interpretations are steeped in history, culture, and philosophical inquiry.

The roots of coincidence can be traced back to ancient civilizations, where the whims of fate and fortune were often attributed to the capriciousness of gods or supernatural forces. In ancient Greece, for example, the concept of "tyche" represented the goddess of fortune, whose unpredictable actions determined the course of human destiny. The Romans venerated Fortuna, the goddess of luck and fate, whose wheel of fortune symbolized the cyclical nature of life's ups and downs.

Throughout history, various religious and philosophical traditions have grappled with the concept of coincidence and its implications for human existence. In Hinduism, the notion of "karma" suggests that actions have consequences that unfold over time, leading to seemingly coincidental outcomes that reflect one's past deeds. In Buddhist philosophy, the concept of "dependent origination" posits that all phenomena are interrelated and interconnected, giving rise to the illusion of coincidence.

During the Renaissance period, the rise of humanism and scientific inquiry spurred a shift in how coincidence was perceived. Rather than attributing events to divine intervention or supernatural forces, thinkers such as Leonardo da Vinci and Galileo Galilei sought to understand the underlying principles governing the natural world. This marked the beginning of a more rationalistic approach to coincidence, rooted in empirical observation and logical reasoning.

In the modern era, the advent of probability theory and statistics provided new tools for understanding and quantifying coincidence. Mathematicians such as Pierre-Simon Laplace and Carl Friedrich Gauss developed probabilistic models to explain random events and patterns of occurrence. These mathematical frameworks laid the groundwork for a more systematic study of coincidence, grounded in empirical data and statistical analysis.

The term "coincidence" itself gained prominence in the 17th century, deriving from the Latin word "coincidere," meaning "to coincide" or "to happen at the same time." Coincidence came to be defined as the occurrence of two or more events that are unrelated by any discernible causal connection but that appear to be meaningfully related.

In the realm of psychology, the concept of coincidence took on new significance with the work of Carl Gustav Jung. Jung introduced the concept of synchronicity in the 1950s, proposing that meaningful coincidences reflect a deeper order or intelligence at work in the universe. Unlike random chance occurrences, synchronistic events carry a sense of significance or resonance, suggesting a hidden connection between inner and outer events.

While coincidence may still evoke skepticism or dismissive attitudes in some circles, its role in shaping human experience and perception cannot be ignored. Whether viewed through the lens of religion, philosophy, science, or psychology, coincidence invites us to contemplate the mysterious interplay of chance and destiny in our lives. As we navigate the currents of existence, may we remain open to the serendipitous encounters and unexpected twists of fate that shape our journey through the labyrinth of time.

Coincidence, that curious dance of chance and circumstance, has captivated human imagination throughout the ages. It's a phenomenon that transcends cultural boundaries and historical epochs, leaving its indelible mark on the fabric of human understanding. From the ancient civilizations of Greece and Rome to the modern era of scientific inquiry, the concept of coincidence has been subject to a myriad of interpretations, each offering a unique perspective on the interplay of randomness and meaning in our lives.

Ancient societies, steeped in myth and legend, often attributed the unfolding of events to the whims of divine entities. In ancient Greece, the goddess Tyche personified fortune, her unpredictable actions believed to shape the destinies of mortals. The Romans revered Fortuna, whose wheel of fortune represented the cyclical nature of luck and fate. These early conceptions of coincidence reflected a belief in a higher order guiding the course of human affairs, a narrative woven with threads of divine intervention and capricious fortune.

Religious and philosophical traditions have long grappled with the complexities of coincidence and its implications for human existence. In Hinduism, the doctrine of karma suggests a cosmic law of cause and effect, wherein actions reverberate through time to shape future outcomes. Likewise, Buddhist philosophy posits the interconnectedness of all phenomena, giving rise to the illusion of coincidental occurrences bound by the intricacies of dependent origination. These ancient teachings offer insights into the deeper layers of meaning underlying seemingly random events, inviting contemplation on the nature of existence and the interconnectedness of all things.

The Renaissance marked a pivotal moment in the evolution of coincidence, as humanist ideals and scientific inquiry began to shape new perspectives on the nature of reality. Figures like Leonardo da Vinci and Galileo Galilei challenged conventional wisdom, advocating for a more empirical approach to understanding the world. Rather than attributing events to supernatural forces, they sought to uncover the underlying principles governing the natural order. This shift towards rationalism laid the groundwork for the emergence of probability theory and statistics, providing a systematic framework for quantifying and analyzing coincidental occurrences.

The 17th century saw the formalization of the concept of coincidence, as scholars began to explore its implications through the lens of mathematics and logic. The term itself, derived from the Latin word "coincidere," came to signify the simultaneous occurrence of unrelated events. Mathematicians like Pierre-Simon Laplace and Carl Friedrich Gauss developed probabilistic models to explain the patterns of chance and randomness observed in the natural world. Their work laid the foundation for a more rigorous understanding of coincidence, grounded in empirical observation and mathematical rigor.

In the realm of psychology, Carl Gustav Jung introduced the concept of synchronicity, proposing a deeper connection between seemingly unrelated events. Unlike random chance occurrences, synchronistic events carry a sense of significance or meaning, hinting at a hidden order underlying the chaos of existence. Jung's theories opened new avenues of exploration into the nature of consciousness and the interconnectedness of the human psyche with the external world.

Today, the study of coincidence continues to evolve, encompassing a diverse array of disciplines and perspectives. From the realms of religion and philosophy to the cutting-edge insights of modern science and psychology, coincidence remains a fertile ground for exploration and discovery. As we navigate the complexities of existence, may we remain open to the serendipitous encounters and unexpected twists of fate that shape our journey through life's labyrinthine paths. For in the dance of coincidence, we glimpse the mysterious workings of the universe, inviting us to ponder the deeper mysteries of existence and our place within it.

Coincidence, with its intricate tapestry of chance and circumstance, invites us to reconsider the boundaries of our understanding and embrace the inherent mysteries of existence. It challenges us to look beyond the surface of events and contemplate the deeper significance that lies beneath. In the grand symphony of life, coincidence serves as a reminder of the interconnectedness of all things, weaving together the threads of past, present, and future into a rich tapestry of meaning and possibility.

From the chance encounters that shape our personal relationships to the seemingly random events that alter the course of history, coincidence surrounds us at every turn. Yet, far from being mere accidents of fate, these seemingly random occurrences often carry profound significance, offering glimpses into the underlying order of the universe. Whether viewed through the lens of science, religion, or philosophy, coincidence invites us to explore the boundaries of our understanding and embrace the inherent mystery of existence.

In the realm of science, coincidence presents a fascinating puzzle for researchers seeking to unravel the mysteries of the cosmos. From the intricate dance of subatomic particles to the vast expanse of the universe itself, the natural world is replete with examples of seemingly random events that defy easy explanation. Yet, beneath the surface chaos lies a hidden order, waiting to be uncovered by the keen eye of the scientist. Through careful observation and rigorous analysis, researchers strive to decipher the underlying principles governing the phenomena of coincidence, shedding light on the fundamental nature of reality itself.

In the realm of religion and spirituality, coincidence takes on a different significance, serving as a potent symbol of divine providence and guidance. Across cultures and faith traditions, believers have long regarded seemingly chance events as signs of a higher power at work in the world. Whether interpreted as the hand of fate or the guiding influence of a benevolent deity, coincidence holds a sacred place in the hearts and minds of the faithful, offering comfort and reassurance in times of uncertainty.

In the realm of philosophy, coincidence serves as a catalyst for existential inquiry, prompting us to question the nature of reality and our place within it. From the ancient Greeks to the existentialist thinkers of the modern era, philosophers have grappled with the profound implications of chance and necessity in shaping human existence. Is life governed by a predetermined fate, or are we free to chart our own course through the vagaries of chance and circumstance? These age-old questions continue to animate philosophical discourse, challenging us to confront the mysteries of existence with courage and humility.

In the realm of psychology, coincidence offers valuable insights into the workings of the human mind and its relationship to the external world. From Carl Jung's concept of synchronicity to modern theories of cognitive bias and perception, psychologists have long been fascinated by the ways in which our brains make sense of seemingly random events. Through careful study and experimentation, researchers seek to unravel the mysteries of coincidence and its impact on human behavior, shedding light on the complex interplay of cognition, emotion, and perception.

Coincidence remains a timeless enigma, inviting us to explore the depths of human understanding and contemplate the mysteries of existence. Whether viewed through the lens of science, religion, philosophy, or psychology, coincidence serves as a potent symbol of the interconnectedness of all things, reminding us of the profound beauty and complexity of the universe in which we dwell. As we journey through life's myriad twists and turns, may we remain open to the serendipitous encounters and unexpected synchronicities that illuminate our path and enrich our understanding of the world around us.

From the chance encounters that shape our personal relationships to the seemingly random events that alter the course of history, coincidence surrounds us at every turn. Yet, far from being mere accidents of fate, these seemingly random occurrences often carry profound significance, offering glimpses into the underlying order of the universe. Whether viewed through the lens of science, religion, or philosophy, coincidence invites us to explore the boundaries of our understanding and embrace the inherent mystery of existence.

In the realm of science, coincidence presents a fascinating puzzle for researchers seeking to unravel the mysteries of the cosmos. From the intricate dance of subatomic particles to the vast expanse of the universe itself, the natural world is replete with examples of seemingly random events that defy easy explanation. Yet, beneath the surface chaos lies a hidden order, waiting to be uncovered by the keen eye of the scientist. Through careful observation and rigorous analysis, researchers strive to decipher the underlying principles governing the phenomena of coincidence, shedding light on the fundamental nature of reality itself.

In the realm of religion and spirituality, coincidence takes on a different significance, serving as a potent symbol of divine providence and guidance. Across cultures and faith traditions, believers have long regarded seemingly chance events as signs of a higher power at work in the world. Whether interpreted as the hand of fate or the guiding influence of a benevolent deity, coincidence holds a sacred place in the hearts and minds of the faithful, offering comfort and reassurance in times of uncertainty.

In the realm of philosophy, coincidence serves as a catalyst for existential inquiry, prompting us to question the nature of reality and our place within it. From the ancient Greeks to the existentialist thinkers of the modern era, philosophers have grappled with the profound implications of chance and necessity in shaping human existence. Is life governed by a predetermined fate, or are we free to chart our own course through the vagaries of chance and circumstance? These age-old questions continue to animate philosophical discourse, challenging us to confront the mysteries of existence with courage and humility.

Coincidence, then, emerges as a multifaceted phenomenon that transcends disciplinary boundaries, inviting us to explore its myriad dimensions and implications. Whether viewed through the lens of science, religion, philosophy, or psychology, coincidence serves as a potent reminder of the mysterious and interconnected nature of existence. As we navigate the complexities of life, may we remain open to the serendipitous encounters and unexpected synchronicities that enrich our journey and deepen our understanding of the world around us.

In the vast landscape of philosophical inquiry, coincidence emerges as a potent catalyst for existential contemplation. Throughout the annals of history, from the intellectual musings of ancient Greek philosophers to the existentialist thinkers of the modern era, the concept of coincidence has served as a fundamental prompt for deep introspection into the nature of reality and our place within it. At its core, coincidence challenges us to grapple with the intricate interplay between chance and necessity in shaping the human experience.

One of the central inquiries that coincidence elicits is the age-old debate surrounding fate versus free will. Does life unfold according to a predetermined script, guided by unseen forces beyond our control, or do we possess the agency to carve out our own destinies amidst the chaos of existence? This philosophical quandary lies at the heart of humanity's quest for meaning and purpose, inviting us to confront the mysteries of our existence with both intellectual rigor and existential humility.

From a philosophical perspective, coincidence serves as a profound reminder of the inherent unpredictability of life. Despite our best efforts to impose order and logic upon the world, we are constantly confronted by the capricious whims of chance and circumstance. Whether it manifests as a chance encounter with a long-lost friend or an unexpected turn of events that alters the trajectory of our lives, coincidence forces us to reckon with the inherent uncertainty that permeates our reality.

The concept of coincidence transcends disciplinary boundaries, permeating various domains of human thought and inquiry. In the realm of science, coincidence challenges our understanding of causality and statistical probability, reminding us of the inherent limitations of our empirical knowledge. In the realm of religion, coincidence often assumes spiritual significance, interpreted as divine intervention or cosmic synchronicity that imbues our lives with deeper meaning and purpose.

Psychologically, coincidence can evoke a range of emotional responses, from wonder and awe to skepticism and disbelief. The human mind is naturally inclined to seek patterns and meaning in the chaos of our experiences, leading us to attribute significance to seemingly random events. This propensity for pattern recognition underscores the intricate relationship between cognition and perception, shaping the way we interpret and make sense of the world around us.

The significance of coincidence lies not in its mere occurrence, but in the meaning we ascribe to it. Whether viewed through a philosophical, scientific, religious, or psychological lens, coincidence serves as a potent symbol of the interconnectedness of all things. In a universe governed by seemingly random fluctuations and chance encounters, we are reminded of our shared humanity and the interconnected tapestry of existence that binds us together.

As we navigate the complexities of life, may we remain open to the serendipitous encounters and unexpected synchronicities that punctuate our journey. For in embracing the mystery of coincidence, we may uncover profound truths about ourselves and the world we inhabit. Through introspection and inquiry, we may come to recognize that, in the grand scheme of things, perhaps there are no mere coincidences—only the interconnected threads of a larger, more enigmatic tapestry of existence.

Chapter 3 - Chance Encounters: Everyday Examples of Synchronicity

Life is replete with moments of serendipity, those unexpected twists of fate that defy rational explanation and leave us pondering the mysteries of existence. From chance encounters with strangers to fortuitous discoveries and uncanny parallels, synchronicity weaves its subtle threads through the fabric of our daily lives. While skeptics may dismiss these occurrences as mere coincidence, those attuned to the nuances of synchronicity recognize them as meaningful reflections of the interconnectedness of all things.

Consider, for instance, the classic example of bumping into an old friend on the street just when you were thinking about them. While skeptics may chalk it up to random chance, proponents of synchronicity see it as a meaningful alignment of inner and outer events. This serendipitous encounter may offer an opportunity for connection, reflection, or shared experience, reaffirming the bonds of friendship and the interconnectedness of human relationships.

Life is a tapestry woven with threads of serendipity, those moments of unexpected delight that defy logic and ignite our sense of wonder. These instances, often dismissed as mere coincidence by skeptics, are cherished by those who recognize the profound interconnectedness of existence.

Think about the times when you've unexpectedly crossed paths with an old friend while strolling down the street. To the skeptic, it might seem like a random occurrence, a chance collision of trajectories in a bustling world. For believers in synchronicity, it's viewed as a harmonious convergence of internal thoughts and external realities.

In the realm of synchronicity, such encounters are not brushed aside as trivial accidents but embraced as meaningful reflections of the universe's intricate design. They serve as reminders that we are not isolated beings navigating through life independently but rather integral parts of a larger cosmic dance.

Consider the depth of meaning embedded within these chance encounters. They offer opportunities for connection, reflection, and sometimes even transformation. A spontaneous conversation with that long-lost friend might spark nostalgia, trigger introspection, or reignite a dormant passion. It's as if the universe conspires to orchestrate these moments, nudging us towards growth and understanding.

Synchronicity extends beyond interpersonal relationships to encompass the realm of personal growth and self-discovery. Think about the times when you stumble upon a book that seems to speak directly to your current challenges, or when a song on the radio echoes the sentiments swirling in your mind. These synchronicities serve as signposts on our journey, guiding us towards insights and revelations that might otherwise elude us.

In the grand tapestry of life, synchronicity adds depth and texture, infusing our existence with a sense of magic and purpose. It invites us to look beyond the surface of things, to perceive the subtle patterns and connections that shape our reality. Whether it's a chance encounter, a timely message, or a serendipitous discovery, each synchronistic moment reminds us that we are part of something greater than ourselves.

But what fuels synchronicity? Is it merely the product of random chance, or is there a deeper intelligence at play? While science may struggle to provide concrete answers, many spiritual traditions and philosophical frameworks offer compelling insights into the nature of synchronicity.

Carl Jung, the renowned Swiss psychiatrist and founder of analytical psychology, introduced the concept of synchronicity to the world. For Jung, synchronicity represented a meaningful coincidence that transcended the limitations of cause and effect. He believed that these synchronistic events were manifestations of the collective unconscious, reflecting deeper archetypal patterns and themes.

From a Jungian perspective, synchronicity arises when the individual's psyche resonates with the underlying currents of the collective unconscious. It's as if our inner world aligns with the broader currents of the cosmos, giving rise to moments of profound significance and resonance.

But synchronicity isn't confined to the realm of psychology; it permeates various aspects of human experience, including art, literature, and spirituality. Think about the recurring motifs and themes found in myths and fairy tales, or the uncanny parallels between different cultures and civilizations. These echoes of synchronicity remind us of the universal truths that transcend time and space.

In essence, synchronicity invites us to embrace the mysteries of existence, to dance with the unknown and marvel at the intricate web of connections that bind us all together. It challenges us to move beyond the narrow confines of rationality and embrace a more expansive view of reality— one that acknowledges the inherent magic and wonder woven into the fabric of life.

So the next time you find yourself marveling at a serendipitous encounter or stumbling upon a synchronistic moment, pause and take notice. For in those fleeting instants, the universe whispers its secrets, inviting you to become an active participant in the unfolding drama of existence.

These synchronicities serve as gentle reminders that there is more to life than meets the eye, urging us to remain open to the infinite possibilities that abound. They encourage us to trust in the unseen forces that guide our journey, knowing that we are always exactly where we need to be, even if it may not seem apparent at first glance.

In a world inundated with noise and distraction, synchronicity acts as a beacon of clarity, cutting through the chaos to reveal glimpses of deeper truth. It teaches us to pay attention to the subtle whispers of intuition, nudging us towards alignment with our true purpose and destiny.

But perhaps the most remarkable aspect of synchronicity is its ability to transcend cultural and linguistic barriers, speaking directly to the core of our shared humanity. Whether you find yourself in a bustling metropolis or a remote village, synchronicity knows no bounds, weaving its magic across time and space.

In the words of author and philosopher Alan Watts, "The coincidence of opposites, the convergence of inner and outer events, the interconnectedness of all things—this is the essence of synchronicity." It is a reminder that everything in the universe is interconnected, that we are all part of a vast, intricate tapestry of existence.

So, as you navigate the ebbs and flows of life, remember to keep your eyes and heart open to the magic of synchronicity. Embrace the moments of serendipity that grace your path, knowing that they are not mere accidents but sacred invitations to awaken to the deeper truths of your being.

In the end, synchronicity invites us to surrender to the mystery, to let go of our need for control and certainty, and to trust in the inherent wisdom of the universe. For in doing so, we open ourselves to a world of endless possibility, where every moment is infused with meaning and purpose, and every encounter is an opportunity for growth and transformation.

It is through embracing synchronicity that we can truly experience the richness and depth of life. Rather than viewing the world through a lens of skepticism or cynicism, we can choose to approach each day with a sense of wonder and curiosity, eager to uncover the hidden connections that lie beneath the surface.

In essence, synchronicity invites us to cultivate a deeper relationship with the universe, one that is based on trust, intuition, and a willingness to surrender to the unknown. It encourages us to let go of our preconceived notions and to embrace the unfolding journey with an open heart and mind.

Synchronicity serves as a potent reminder of our interconnectedness with all beings and phenomena. It reminds us that we are not separate, isolated entities but rather integral parts of a vast and intricate web of life. Each synchronistic moment is a testament to the fact that we are all inextricably linked, bound together by the invisible threads of existence.

In a world that often feels fragmented and divided, synchronicity offers a glimmer of hope and unity. It reminds us that beneath the surface of our differences lies a deeper truth—one of shared humanity and interconnectedness. When we open ourselves to the magic of synchronicity, we allow ourselves to see beyond the illusions of separation and division, and to recognize the inherent beauty and interconnectedness of all things.

Synchronicity invites us to become active participants in the unfolding story of the cosmos. It encourages us to embrace the mysteries of existence with open arms and to dance with the rhythm of life itself. In doing so, we not only enrich our own lives but also contribute to the collective tapestry of consciousness, weaving new threads of meaning and significance into the fabric of reality.

So, the next time you experience a moment of synchronicity, whether it's a chance encounter with a stranger or a serendipitous twist of fate, pause and take notice. Allow yourself to be swept away by the magic of the moment, knowing that you are being guided by forces far greater than yourself. And remember, in the grand symphony of existence, each synchronistic moment is a note, adding its unique melody to the eternal song of the universe.

Synchronicity, with its subtle yet undeniable presence in our lives, encourages us to shift our perspective from one of skepticism to one of receptivity. It teaches us to embrace uncertainty and ambiguity, recognizing that within the realm of the unknown lies the potential for profound insight and revelation.

Furthermore, synchronicity invites us to engage with the world around us in a more mindful and attentive manner. By cultivating awareness of the synchronistic patterns that unfold in our lives, we become attuned to the underlying currents of meaning and significance that flow through our experiences.

Synchronicity serves as a catalyst for personal growth and transformation. When we open ourselves to the messages and insights contained within synchronistic events, we create space for profound shifts in consciousness to occur. These moments of alignment with the deeper currents of existence have the power to catalyze profound shifts in our perception of reality, leading to greater clarity, insight, and wisdom.

In essence, synchronicity invites us to become active participants in the co-creative process of reality itself. It reminds us that we are not passive observers of our lives but active agents in the ongoing evolution of consciousness. By embracing synchronicity, we open ourselves to a world of infinite possibility, where every moment is infused with meaning and purpose.

Synchronicity serves as a reminder of the inherent magic and mystery of existence. It challenges us to look beyond the surface of things and to recognize the interconnectedness of all phenomena. In doing so, we awaken to the profound truth that we are not separate from the universe but rather integral participants in the grand symphony of life.

Embracing synchronicity fosters a deep sense of gratitude and reverence for the interconnectedness of all beings and events. It encourages us to approach each encounter and experience with an open heart and a sense of wonder, recognizing the inherent beauty and significance in even the most seemingly mundane moments.

Synchronicity also serves as a powerful reminder of the importance of trust and surrender in our lives. When we relinquish our need for control and allow ourselves to flow with the currents of synchronicity, we open ourselves to a world of limitless possibility. We begin to trust in the inherent wisdom of the universe, knowing that everything unfolds according to a greater plan beyond our comprehension.

Furthermore, synchronicity invites us to cultivate a deeper relationship with our intuition and inner guidance. By paying attention to the subtle whispers of our inner voice and following the signs and synchronicities that appear in our lives, we align ourselves with the flow of divine guidance and wisdom.

In essence, synchronicity is a reflection of the interconnectedness, harmony, and beauty that permeate the fabric of existence. It is a gentle reminder that we are all interconnected, and that every thought, action, and experience ripples out and affects the greater whole.

As we continue to journey through life, may we remain open to the magic of synchronicity and embrace the mystery and wonder that it holds. For in doing so, we awaken to the profound truth that we are not separate from the universe, but rather integral participants in the cosmic dance of creation.

Synchronicity serves as a bridge between the conscious and unconscious realms of the psyche, inviting us to explore the depths of our own inner landscapes. When we attune ourselves to the synchronistic events that unfold in our lives, we gain valuable insights into our subconscious desires, fears, and patterns.

By paying attention to the recurring themes and symbols that emerge in our synchronistic experiences, we can uncover hidden aspects of ourselves and gain a deeper understanding of our own motivations and behaviors. In this way, synchronicity becomes a powerful tool for self-discovery and personal growth, guiding us on a journey of transformation and evolution.

Furthermore, synchronicity reminds us of the importance of being present and mindful in our daily lives. When we are fully present and attentive to the synchronistic events that occur around us, we open ourselves to a deeper level of awareness and connection with the world around us. We begin to see the beauty and magic that surrounds us in every moment, and we develop a greater appreciation for the richness and complexity of life.

Synchronicity invites us to embrace the inherent mystery and uncertainty of existence, trusting in the unfolding of the universe and surrendering to the flow of life. When we allow ourselves to be guided by synchronicity, we align ourselves with the natural rhythms of creation and open ourselves to a world of infinite possibility and potential.

Synchronicity is a profound and mysterious phenomenon that offers us glimpses into the interconnectedness and beauty of the universe. By embracing synchronicity in our lives, we can deepen our connection with ourselves, with others, and with the world around us, and embark on a journey of self-discovery, growth, and transformation.

The exploration of synchronicity leads us to contemplate the nature of time and causality. In synchronistic experiences, the linear concept of cause and effect seems to dissolve, giving way to a more holistic understanding of how events unfold. Rather than viewing time as a linear progression from past to future, synchronicity invites us to consider the possibility of a timeless, interconnected web of existence where past, present, and future coalesce.

This perspective challenges our conventional notions of reality and invites us to expand our awareness beyond the limitations of linear thinking. It encourages us to see the world in a more fluid and dynamic way, where seemingly disparate events are interconnected in ways that defy logical explanation.

Furthermore, the study of synchronicity has practical applications in fields such as psychology, therapy, and personal development. Therapists and counselors may use synchronicity as a tool for helping clients explore their unconscious motivations, patterns, and beliefs. By paying attention to synchronistic events in therapy sessions, clients can gain valuable insights into their inner worlds and accelerate the process of self-discovery and healing.

Individuals engaged in personal development and spiritual growth often use synchronicity as a guide on their journey. By cultivating a receptive and attentive mindset, they are able to recognize and interpret the signs and symbols that appear in their lives, gaining clarity and direction as they navigate their path.

In essence, the study of synchronicity invites us to embrace a more expansive and interconnected view of reality. It challenges us to look beyond the surface of things and to recognize the deeper patterns and meanings that underlie our experiences. By embracing synchronicity in our lives, we open ourselves to a world of infinite possibility and potential, where every moment is imbued with significance and every encounter is an opportunity for growth and transformation.

Delving into the realm of synchronicity prompts us to question the nature of consciousness itself. Synchronistic experiences often defy conventional explanations, leading us to ponder the existence of a deeper, underlying intelligence or universal consciousness. Could it be that synchronicity is not merely a random occurrence, but rather a manifestation of a larger, interconnected field of consciousness in which we all participate?

This line of inquiry opens up a vast and profound philosophical exploration into the nature of reality. It challenges us to reconsider our understanding of the boundaries between self and other, individual and collective, material and spiritual. Synchronicity beckons us to explore the interconnectedness of all things and to contemplate our place within the larger tapestry of existence.

Furthermore, the study of synchronicity has implications for fields beyond psychology and philosophy, extending into areas such as quantum physics and neuroscience. In quantum physics, the concept of entanglement suggests that particles can become interconnected in such a way that the state of one particle is instantaneously influenced by the state of another, regardless of the distance between them. This phenomenon resonates with the interconnectedness observed in synchronistic experiences, hinting at a deeper relationship between consciousness and the fabric of reality.

Research in neuroscience has begun to shed light on the neural mechanisms underlying synchronicity. Studies have shown that certain brain regions associated with perception, memory, and emotion may play a role in the processing of synchronistic events. By investigating the neural correlates of synchronicity, scientists hope to gain a better understanding of how these experiences arise and how they may impact our perception of reality.

The exploration of synchronicity opens up a fascinating and multifaceted inquiry into the nature of reality, consciousness, and the interconnectedness of all things. It challenges us to expand our awareness beyond the confines of conventional thinking and to embrace a more holistic and interconnected view of the world. As we continue to unravel the mysteries of synchronicity, we may find ourselves drawn into a deeper understanding of the fundamental nature of existence itself.

Chapter 4 - The Psychology of Meaning: Jung's Archetypes and Collective Unconscious

In the realm of psychology, few figures loom as large as Carl Gustav Jung, whose pioneering work delved into the depths of the human psyche and its collective dimensions. Central to Jung's framework is the concept of the collective unconscious, a reservoir of archetypal symbols and patterns shared by all humanity. Within this vast repository of the unconscious mind lie the archetypes, universal symbols and motifs that shape our thoughts, emotions, and behaviors.

Jung believed that the collective unconscious serves as a bridge between the personal and the universal, connecting individual experiences to the broader currents of human history and culture. At the heart of this collective realm are the archetypes, primordial images and themes that recur across cultures and epochs, reflecting fundamental aspects of the human condition. From the mother archetype, symbolizing nurturing and fertility, to the shadow archetype, representing the repressed and unconscious aspects of the self, these archetypes serve as symbolic templates that inform our perceptions and motivations.

One of Jung's most influential concepts is that of synchronicity, which he introduced in the 1950s as a way of understanding meaningful coincidences that cannot be explained by traditional notions of causality. Jung proposed that synchronistic events arise from the interconnectedness of the collective unconscious, where archetypal patterns and universal symbols intersect with individual lives. For Jung, synchronicity represents a convergence of inner and outer events, reflecting the deeper order and intelligence at work in the universe.

To illustrate the interplay between archetypes, the collective unconscious, and synchronicity, consider the example of the hero's journey, a common mythic motif found in cultures around the world. The hero's journey archetype represents the quest for self-discovery and transformation, in which the protagonist embarks on a perilous adventure, faces trials and tribulations, and ultimately emerges transformed. This archetype resonates deeply with the human psyche, reflecting our innate desire for growth, adventure, and self-realization.

Synchronistic experiences often mirror the themes and symbols of archetypal narratives, serving as symbolic reflections of the hero's journey in our own lives. Whether it's a chance encounter that leads to a transformative insight or a dream that provides guidance on our life path, synchronicity invites us to recognize the archetypal patterns at play and to heed the wisdom they offer.

Jung's concept of the collective unconscious and its archetypal contents has profound implications for psychology, mythology, and cultural studies. By exploring the symbolic language of the unconscious mind, we gain insights into the deeper layers of human experience and the universal themes that bind us together as a species. Whether expressed through dreams, myths, or synchronistic encounters, the archetypes remind us of our shared humanity and our interconnectedness with the cosmos.

Jung posited that the collective unconscious acts as a bridge, connecting the personal experiences of individuals to the broader tapestry of human history and culture. Within this collective realm, the archetypes reign supreme – timeless symbols and motifs that transcend geographical and temporal boundaries. From the nurturing embrace of the mother archetype to the enigmatic depths of the shadow archetype, these universal symbols serve as the building blocks of the human psyche, shaping our perceptions and motivations in profound ways.

To elucidate the interplay between archetypes, the collective unconscious, and synchronicity, one need only consider the archetype of the hero's journey. Found in mythologies across cultures, the hero's journey embodies the quest for self-discovery and transformation. Through trials and tribulations, the protagonist undergoes profound inner growth, ultimately emerging transformed. This archetype resonates deeply with the human psyche, encapsulating our innate yearning for adventure and self-realization.

Synchronistic experiences often mirror the themes and symbols of archetypal narratives, serving as symbolic reflections of the hero's journey in our own lives. Whether it's an unexpected encounter that leads to a moment of enlightenment or a dream that offers guidance on our life path, synchronicity beckons us to heed the wisdom encoded within these archetypal patterns.

Jung's conceptualization of the collective unconscious and its archetypal contents holds far-reaching implications for psychology, mythology, and cultural studies alike. By deciphering the symbolic language of the unconscious mind, we gain access to the profound depths of human experience and the universal themes that bind us together as a species. Whether manifested through dreams, myths, or synchronistic encounters, the archetypes serve as timeless reminders of our shared humanity and our interconnectedness with the cosmos.

In essence, Jung's enduring legacy lies in his profound understanding of the human psyche's collective dimensions. Through his exploration of archetypes, the collective unconscious, and synchronicity, he illuminated the intricate tapestry of the human experience, offering insights that continue to resonate across disciplines and generations. As we navigate the complexities of existence, Jung's teachings serve as a guiding light, reminding us of the profound interconnectedness that lies at the heart of our shared humanity.

Jung's contributions to psychology extend beyond theoretical frameworks, permeating into practical applications and therapeutic modalities. His concepts have found resonance in fields ranging from psychotherapy to literature, art, and even popular culture. The archetypes, for instance, serve as invaluable tools in psychotherapy, enabling individuals to explore and integrate unconscious material, leading to personal growth and individuation.

Jung's emphasis on the symbolic language of the unconscious has influenced literary and artistic movements, inspiring creators to delve into the depths of the human psyche. Writers, artists, and filmmakers often draw upon archetypal motifs to craft narratives that resonate with universal themes and resonate deeply with audiences across cultures.

In the realm of cultural studies, Jung's ideas have sparked inquiries into the enduring relevance of mythological motifs and archetypal narratives in contemporary society. Scholars explore how ancient myths and archetypes continue to shape our collective consciousness, influencing everything from political ideologies to consumer behavior.

Furthermore, Jung's concept of synchronicity has implications beyond psychology, intersecting with fields such as philosophy, physics, and spirituality. Philosophers ponder the nature of coincidence and the underlying interconnectedness of all things, while physicists explore parallels between synchronicity and quantum entanglement, suggesting a deeper unity underlying the fabric of reality.

Spiritual traditions around the world resonate with Jung's notion of synchronicity, viewing it as evidence of a higher intelligence or cosmic order at work in the universe. Practices such as meditation, ritual, and divination are often employed to attune oneself to synchronistic occurrences and gain insight into the underlying patterns of existence.

Carl Jung's legacy continues to reverberate across diverse domains, from psychology to literature, art, philosophy, and spirituality. His exploration of the collective unconscious, archetypes, and synchronicity has enriched our understanding of the human experience and offered profound insights into the mysteries of existence. As we navigate the complexities of modern life, Jung's teachings serve as a beacon, guiding us toward greater self-awareness, connection, and meaning in a world imbued with symbolic significance and synchronistic possibilities.

Jung's influence extends into modern therapeutic approaches, where his concepts are integrated into various forms of depth psychology and analytical therapy. Practitioners utilize techniques such as dream analysis, active imagination, and symbol work to help clients explore the depths of their psyches and uncover unconscious patterns that may be influencing their lives.

Jung's emphasis on the individuation process, the journey toward wholeness and self-realization, has profound implications for personal development and spiritual growth. By embracing the diverse aspects of the self, both conscious and unconscious, individuals can embark on a path of integration and transformation, leading to a more authentic and fulfilling life.

In the realm of education, Jung's ideas have influenced pedagogical approaches that recognize the importance of honoring students' individual differences and fostering a holistic understanding of learning. Educators draw upon archetypal motifs and mythic narratives to engage students' imaginations and cultivate deeper insights into the human experience.

Jung's work also resonates with contemporary discussions surrounding identity, diversity, and inclusivity. By acknowledging the multiplicity of archetypal energies within each individual and within society as a whole, Jungian psychology offers a framework for embracing the richness of human diversity while also recognizing the underlying unity that connects us all.

Furthermore, Jung's concepts have sparked interdisciplinary dialogues that transcend traditional boundaries, fostering collaborations between psychologists, anthropologists, theologians, and philosophers. These cross-disciplinary exchanges enrich our understanding of the human condition and provide new perspectives on age-old questions about the nature of consciousness, reality, and the divine.

In the digital age, Jung's ideas have found expression in online communities and virtual spaces where individuals explore themes of self-discovery, personal growth, and spiritual awakening. Blogs, podcasts, and social media platforms serve as forums for sharing synchronistic experiences, discussing archetypal symbolism, and engaging in dialogues that bridge the gap between the personal and the collective unconscious.

In essence, Carl Jung's legacy continues to evolve and adapt to the ever-changing landscape of human experience. His insights into the depths of the psyche, the universality of mythic motifs, and the meaningfulness of synchronistic events offer profound wisdom for navigating the complexities of contemporary life. As we continue to grapple with existential questions and seek deeper connections with ourselves and the world around us, Jung's teachings serve as a source of inspiration and guidance, illuminating the path toward greater self-awareness, integration, and wholeness.

Jung's influence extends into various branches of psychotherapy, including analytical psychology, where therapists engage clients in a process of exploring unconscious dynamics and integrating conflicting aspects of the psyche. Through techniques such as active imagination and the exploration of dreams, individuals can uncover hidden patterns and symbols that offer insight into their inner world.

Beyond the realm of therapy, Jung's ideas have permeated popular culture, inspiring countless books, films, and television shows that explore themes of personal transformation, spiritual awakening, and the quest for meaning. From the hero's journey archetype in epic fantasy sagas to the symbolism of the shadow in psychological thrillers, Jungian concepts continue to captivate audiences and spark reflections on the human condition.

In academia, Jung's theories have sparked interdisciplinary research projects that investigate the intersections of psychology, mythology, anthropology, and religious studies. Scholars explore how archetypal motifs manifest in different cultural contexts, shedding light on the universal themes that underpin human experience and the ways in which they shape collective identity and behavior.

Jung's legacy also reverberates in the field of organizational development, where his insights into the dynamics of the collective unconscious have informed approaches to leadership, team dynamics, and organizational culture. By recognizing the influence of archetypal patterns and unconscious processes within groups, organizations can foster greater cohesion, creativity, and innovation.

Jung's ideas have inspired innovative approaches to environmental psychology and Eco psychology, which explore the psychological relationship between individuals and the natural world. By recognizing the symbolic significance of nature and the archetypal motifs inherent in ecological systems, these fields offer insights into the ways in which our connection to the environment shapes our mental health and well-being.

In the realm of spirituality, Jung's concepts continue to inform practices such as meditation, dream work, and ritual, providing frameworks for exploring the depths of the soul and cultivating a deeper sense of connection to the divine. Jungian analysts and spiritual seekers alike draw upon archetypal symbolism to navigate the inner landscape and uncover the sacred dimensions of human existence.

Carl Jung's enduring legacy lies in his profound exploration of the human psyche and its collective dimensions. His insights into the nature of archetypes, synchronicity, and the unconscious continue to inspire individuals across diverse fields and disciplines, offering pathways to greater self-awareness, personal growth, and cultural transformation. As we continue to grapple with the complexities of the modern world, Jung's teachings serve as a beacon of wisdom, guiding us toward a deeper understanding of ourselves and our place in the universe.

Furthermore, Jung's influence extends into the realm of art therapy, where his concepts provide a framework for exploring creativity, symbolism, and the healing potential of artistic expression. By engaging in artistic processes, individuals can tap into the unconscious mind, accessing deeper layers of emotion and meaning that may be difficult to express verbally. Art therapy offers a safe and supportive space for individuals to explore their inner world, integrate conflicting emotions, and foster self-discovery and growth.

Besides, Jung's ideas have shaped the field of depth coaching, where practitioners draw upon archetypal imagery and symbolism to guide clients in navigating life transitions, clarifying goals, and unlocking their creative potential. Through techniques such as visualization, journaling, and metaphorical exploration, clients can gain insight into unconscious patterns and develop a deeper understanding of themselves and their aspirations.

Jung's concepts also find resonance in the study of symbolism and mythology, where scholars explore the ways in which ancient myths and archetypal motifs continue to influence contemporary culture and consciousness. By delving into the symbolic language of myths, fairy tales, and religious texts, researchers uncover universal themes and archetypal patterns that speak to the deepest aspects of the human psyche.

Jung's work has inspired the development of transpersonal psychology, a branch of psychology that explores the spiritual dimensions of human experience and the interconnectedness of all life. Transpersonal psychologists use Jungian ideas like individuation and the collective unconscious to help people break free from egoic constraints and reach higher levels of consciousness.

In the realm of cultural psychology, Jung's ideas have contributed to our understanding of cultural identity, symbolism, and ritual. By examining the ways in which different cultures express and embody archetypal themes, researchers gain insight into the universal aspects of human experience as well as the cultural variations that shape our perceptions and behaviors.

Furthermore, Jung's concepts have been applied in the field of depth sociology, where researchers explore the collective dimensions of society and culture. By analyzing societal myths, symbols, and rituals, sociologists gain insight into the underlying dynamics that shape social structures, values, and norms.

Carl Jung's legacy extends far beyond the confines of psychology, permeating into numerous fields and disciplines. His insights into the collective unconscious, archetypal symbolism, and synchronicity continue to inspire individuals across diverse domains, offering pathways to deeper self-understanding, personal growth, and cultural transformation. As we continue to explore the mysteries of the human psyche and the interconnectedness of all life, Jung's teachings serve as a guiding light, illuminating the path toward greater wholeness, integration, and harmony.

Jung's profound influence extends into the realm of literature, where his ideas have inspired countless authors to explore themes of the unconscious, archetypal symbolism, and the human quest for meaning. From classic works of fiction to contemporary novels, Jungian motifs and concepts often serve as underlying themes, inviting readers to delve into the depths of the psyche and ponder existential questions about identity, purpose, and the nature of reality.

Jung's insights have shaped the field of narrative therapy, where therapists utilize storytelling and metaphor to help clients make sense of their experiences and construct empowering narratives for their lives. By reframing personal stories within archetypal frameworks, individuals can gain a deeper understanding of their struggles and strengths, leading to greater resilience and self-compassion.

In the realm of education, Jung's ideas have influenced holistic approaches to teaching and learning that honor the diverse ways in which students perceive and process information. Educators draw upon archetypal themes and symbolic imagery to engage students' imaginations and foster creative thinking, empowering them to explore the depths of their own consciousness and cultivate a lifelong love of learning.

Furthermore, Jung's concepts have inspired innovative approaches to leadership development, where executives and organizational leaders explore the unconscious dynamics that influence group dynamics, decision-making processes, and organizational culture. By embracing the symbolic language of the collective unconscious, leaders can cultivate greater self-awareness, empathy, and authenticity, fostering environments that are conducive to collaboration, innovation, and growth.

Jung's ideas also find resonance in the field of eco-psychology, where researchers explore the psychological relationship between individuals and the natural world. By recognizing the symbolic significance of nature and the archetypal motifs inherent in ecological systems, eco-psychologists offer insights into the ways in which our connection to the environment shapes our mental health, well-being, and sense of belonging in the world.

Jung's concepts have been applied in the realm of holistic health and wellness, where practitioners draw upon archetypal imagery and symbolic rituals to promote healing and transformation. From mindfulness practices to expressive arts therapies, individuals can explore the depths of their own psyche and connect with the healing energies of the collective unconscious, leading to greater vitality, resilience, and wholeness.

Carl Jung's legacy continues to inspire individuals across diverse fields and disciplines, offering profound insights into the mysteries of the human psyche and the interconnectedness of all life. Whether applied in therapy, education, leadership, or personal growth, Jung's teachings serve as a timeless reminder of the profound wisdom encoded within the depths of the unconscious mind. As we continue to explore the depths of human consciousness and the mysteries of existence, Jung's insights offer a guiding light, illuminating the path toward greater self-awareness, integration, and harmony with ourselves, each other, and the world around us.

Chapter 5 - The Quantum Field: Exploring the Physics of Synchronicity

The realm of quantum physics is a strange and wondrous domain, where particles can exist in multiple states simultaneously, and reality is shaped by the observer's consciousness. At the heart of this enigmatic landscape lies the quantum field, a vast and dynamic matrix of energy that underlies all of existence. In recent years, physicists have begun to explore the potential connections between quantum mechanics and the mysterious phenomenon of synchronicity.

Central to the quantum worldview is the concept of nonlocality, which suggests that particles can become entangled in such a way that their states are correlated regardless of the distance between them. This phenomenon, known as quantum entanglement, violates classical notions of causality and suggests a deeper interconnectedness that transcends the boundaries of space and time. Some physicists have speculated that quantum entanglement may provide a potential mechanism for synchronicity, whereby meaningful coincidences arise from the entangled nature of reality.

Furthermore, the role of consciousness in quantum mechanics has sparked intriguing parallels with Jung's concept of synchronicity. According to quantum consciousness theories, the observer's consciousness plays a fundamental role in shaping reality, collapsing the wave function and determining the outcome of quantum events. This intimate connection between consciousness and the quantum realm echoes Jung's notion of synchronicity, where inner states of mind are reflected in outer events.

In light of these developments, the bridge between quantum physics and synchronicity becomes increasingly apparent. Both frameworks challenge our classical notions of space, time, and causality, pointing to a reality that is far more complex and interconnected than we previously imagined. While the mysteries of the quantum field may continue to elude our understanding, its potential implications for synchronicity offer tantalizing avenues for exploration.

From a quantum perspective, synchronicity may be viewed as a manifestation of the underlying entanglement and connectivity that permeate the fabric of reality. Rather than isolated events occurring in isolation, synchronistic experiences arise from the intricate dance of particles and waves within the quantum field. By exploring the physics of synchronicity, we gain a deeper appreciation for the mysterious ways in which the universe unfolds and the profound interplay between mind and matter.

Chapter 6 - Entanglement and Connectivity: Quantum Mechanics in Everyday Life

The mysteries of quantum mechanics may seem far removed from our everyday experiences, confined to the realm of laboratories and theoretical debates. The principles of quantum physics have profound implications for our understanding of reality, consciousness, and the interconnectedness of all things. From the bizarre phenomenon of quantum entanglement to the subtle influences of the quantum field, the insights of quantum mechanics offer a new lens through which to view the world around us.

At the heart of quantum mechanics is the concept of entanglement, whereby particles become correlated in such a way that the state of one instantaneously influences the state of another, regardless of the distance between them. This phenomenon, famously described by Albert Einstein as "spooky action at a distance," challenges our classical notions of causality and suggests a deeper interconnectedness that transcends the boundaries of space and time.

While quantum entanglement may seem like a strange and esoteric concept, its implications extend far beyond the realm of physics. In recent years, researchers have begun to explore the potential connections between quantum entanglement and synchronicity, the mysterious phenomenon of meaningful coincidences that seem to defy conventional explanations. Some scientists have proposed that synchronicity may arise from the entangled nature of reality, whereby events become correlated in ways that transcend our ordinary understanding of cause and effect.

Furthermore, the role of consciousness in quantum mechanics has sparked intriguing parallels with the concept of synchronicity. According to quantum consciousness theories, the observer's consciousness plays a fundamental role in shaping reality, collapsing the wave function and determining the outcome of quantum events. This intimate connection between consciousness and the quantum realm echoes the notion of synchronicity, where inner states of mind are reflected in outer events.

In everyday life, we may encounter synchronistic experiences that hint at the underlying entanglement and connectivity of the quantum realm. Whether it's a chance encounter that leads to a life-changing insight or a serendipitous event that alters the course of our destiny, synchronicity invites us to recognize the hidden patterns and connections that weave through the fabric of reality. By embracing the insights of quantum mechanics, we gain a deeper appreciation for the mysterious ways in which the universe unfolds and the profound interplay between mind and matter.

The mysteries of quantum mechanics often appear distant from our daily lives, seemingly confined to laboratories and theoretical discussions. The principles of quantum physics hold profound implications for our comprehension of reality, consciousness, and the interconnectedness of all existence. From the enigmatic phenomenon of quantum entanglement to the subtle influences of the quantum field, the revelations of quantum mechanics provide a fresh perspective on the world around us.

At its core, quantum mechanics revolves around the notion of entanglement. This concept describes how particles become correlated in a manner where the state of one instantaneously influences the state of another, irrespective of the physical separation between them. Albert Einstein famously referred to this as "spooky action at a distance," challenging traditional causal frameworks and suggesting a profound interconnectedness that transcends conventional boundaries.

While quantum entanglement might initially appear obscure and complex, its implications extend well beyond the confines of physics. In recent times, researchers have delved into potential links between quantum entanglement and synchronicity – the inexplicable occurrences of meaningful coincidences defying rational explanations. Some scientists propose that synchronicity could emerge from the entangled nature of reality, where events become correlated in ways that surpass ordinary cause-and-effect relationships.

The intersection of consciousness and quantum mechanics has drawn intriguing parallels with the concept of synchronicity. Quantum consciousness theories posit that the observer's consciousness plays a pivotal role in shaping reality, collapsing the wave function and determining the outcomes of quantum events. This intimate relationship between consciousness and the quantum realm resonates with the idea of synchronicity, where inner mental states manifest in external events.

In our everyday lives, we may encounter synchronistic experiences hinting at the underlying entanglement and interconnectedness of the quantum realm. Whether it's an unexpected encounter leading to a profound insight or a serendipitous event altering our life's trajectory, synchronicity beckons us to acknowledge the concealed patterns and connections interwoven within the fabric of reality. Embracing the insights of quantum mechanics offers us a deeper understanding of the mysterious unfolding of the universe and the profound interplay between mind and matter.

The enigmatic nature of quantum mechanics often leads to contemplation about the fundamental structure of reality. Quantum physicists grapple with concepts that defy classical intuitions, such as particles existing in multiple states simultaneously or the probabilistic nature of quantum events. These perplexing aspects challenge conventional notions of determinism and underscore the inherent uncertainty at the heart of quantum theory.

One of the most fascinating aspects of quantum mechanics is its potential to revolutionize technologies. Quantum computing, for instance, harnesses the principles of superposition and entanglement to perform computations exponentially faster than classical computers. This burgeoning field holds promise for tackling complex problems in cryptography, optimization, and scientific simulations, paving the way for unprecedented advancements in various domains.

Quantum mechanics has spurred groundbreaking developments in quantum cryptography, ensuring secure communication channels resistant to eavesdropping and interception. By leveraging the principles of quantum entanglement, quantum cryptography enables the creation of cryptographic keys with unparalleled security, laying the foundation for next-generation encryption protocols essential in an increasingly interconnected world.

Beyond its practical applications, quantum mechanics also offers profound insights into the nature of reality and human consciousness. The concept of wave-particle duality, for instance, suggests that particles exhibit both wave-like and particle-like behavior depending on how they are observed—an observation that challenges our intuitive understanding of matter. The uncertainty principle, formulated by Werner Heisenberg, asserts that there are inherent limits to our ability to simultaneously measure certain pairs of physical properties, highlighting the inherent indeterminacy woven into the fabric of reality.

In the realm of cosmology, quantum mechanics intersects with the study of the universe's origins and evolution. The concept of quantum fluctuations posits that tiny fluctuations in the quantum vacuum during the early universe's inflationary period gave rise to the seeds of cosmic structure, eventually leading to the formation of galaxies, stars, and planets. This cosmic dance of quantum probabilities underscores the intricate interplay between the microscopic realm of quantum physics and the vast expanse of the cosmos.

Furthermore, the philosophical implications of quantum mechanics have sparked debates about the nature of free will, determinism, and the role of consciousness in shaping reality. Some argue that quantum indeterminacy introduces genuine randomness into the universe, providing room for free will to operate beyond the constraints of deterministic causality. Others contend that while quantum mechanics introduces probabilistic uncertainties, it does not necessarily imply a departure from causal determinism, raising profound questions about the nature of choice and agency in a quantum world.

Quantum mechanics transcends its status as a mere scientific theory, offering profound insights into the nature of reality, consciousness, and the interconnectedness of all existence. From the enigmatic phenomena of quantum entanglement and wave-particle duality to the practical applications of quantum computing and cryptography, the implications of quantum mechanics reverberate across diverse fields and disciplines. As we continue to unravel the mysteries of the quantum realm, we embark on a journey towards a deeper understanding of the universe and our place within it.

In the vast and intricate tapestry of cosmology, where the study of the universe's origins and evolution unfolds, quantum mechanics emerges as a fascinating intersection. It delves into the profound implications of the microscopic realm, intertwining with the expansive expanse of the cosmos. At the heart of this convergence lies the concept of quantum fluctuations, a notion that proposes the existence of minute perturbations within the quantum vacuum during the universe's primordial inflationary epoch. These fluctuations, though imperceptible on a macroscopic scale, are believed to have seeded the formation of cosmic structures, laying the groundwork for the emergence of galaxies, stars, and planets.

The narrative of cosmic evolution becomes a dance of quantum probabilities, where the seemingly deterministic pathways of celestial bodies are influenced by the inherent randomness of quantum mechanics. This intricate interplay challenges our perceptions of causality and determinism, inviting contemplation on the fundamental nature of the universe. It leads us to question whether the universe operates under the sway of deterministic laws or if genuine randomness, introduced by quantum indeterminacy, imbues it with an element of unpredictability.

Philosophical discourse surrounding quantum mechanics delves even deeper, touching upon existential inquiries about free will, determinism, and the role of consciousness in shaping reality. Advocates of free will find solace in the uncertainty inherent in quantum mechanics, viewing it as a realm where choices are not bound by deterministic causality. They argue that the probabilistic nature of quantum phenomena allows for genuine agency, transcending the rigid constraints of predetermined fate.

Conversely, skeptics challenge this perspective, suggesting that while quantum mechanics introduces probabilistic uncertainties, it does not necessarily relinquish the reins of determinism. They posit that underlying deterministic principles may still govern the unfolding of events, even amidst the quantum fuzziness. This nuanced debate illuminates the complex relationship between quantum mechanics and philosophical concepts, prompting introspection into the nature of choice, agency, and consciousness in a quantum reality.

Yet, beyond the philosophical musings lie tangible applications and technological marvels born out of our understanding of quantum mechanics. Quantum entanglement, a phenomenon where particles become inextricably linked regardless of distance, holds promise for revolutionizing communication and computing technologies. The enigmatic nature of wave-particle duality has spurred innovations in quantum computing, where qubits harness superposition and entanglement to perform calculations at unprecedented speeds.

The realm of quantum cryptography offers secure communication channels resistant to eavesdropping, leveraging the principles of quantum mechanics to safeguard sensitive information. These practical applications underscore the transformative potential of quantum mechanics, transcending theoretical speculation to redefine the technological landscape of the future.

In the grand tapestry of human exploration, the journey into the quantum realm represents a quest for understanding that transcends disciplinary boundaries. It is a voyage fueled by curiosity, driven by the desire to unravel the mysteries of existence and unlock the secrets of the universe. As we peer into the quantum abyss, we are confronted with a reality that defies intuition, challenging our preconceived notions of space, time, and causality.

Yet, amid the uncertainty and complexity, there is a profound beauty in the elegance of quantum mechanics—a beauty that transcends mathematical formalism and theoretical abstraction. It is a beauty that speaks to the interconnectedness of all things, weaving a web of cosmic relationships that bind the fabric of reality together.

Quantum mechanics stands as a testament to the boundless depths of human inquiry, offering not only a glimpse into the nature of reality but also a reflection of our own consciousness. It is a journey of exploration and discovery, where the boundaries between science and philosophy blur, and the mysteries of the universe beckon us to delve deeper. As we navigate this wondrous realm, we embark on a voyage of enlightenment, guided by the timeless pursuit of knowledge and the inexorable pull of curiosity.

The quest to comprehend the quantum realm is far from over; it is an ongoing expedition into the heart of existence itself. With each new discovery, we peel back another layer of the cosmic onion, revealing ever more intricate patterns and relationships. Yet, for all our advancements, the quantum world remains elusive, its mysteries tantalizingly out of reach. It is a realm where paradox reigns supreme, where particles exist in a state of superposition, occupying multiple states simultaneously until observed. This phenomenon, known as the observer effect, highlights the profound influence of consciousness on the behavior of quantum systems, blurring the lines between observer and observed.

The concept of quantum entanglement, famously described by Einstein as "spooky action at a distance," continues to defy our conventional understanding of space and time. It suggests that particles can become entwined in such a way that the state of one instantaneously influences the state of the other, regardless of the distance separating them. This phenomenon challenges our intuitive notions of causality and locality, hinting at a deeper interconnectedness woven into the very fabric of reality.

As we navigate the labyrinthine corridors of the quantum realm, we are confronted with the limitations of our own perception. Our classical intuitions, honed by millennia of evolution in a macroscopic world, falter in the face of quantum weirdness. It is a humbling reminder of the vastness of the unknown, of the limitless frontiers that lie beyond the boundaries of our current understanding.

Yet, in our pursuit of knowledge, we press onward, driven by an insatiable curiosity to unravel the mysteries of the cosmos. With each experiment, each observation, we inch closer to unlocking the secrets of the quantum realm, illuminating the dark recesses of existence with the light of human understanding. And though the journey may be fraught with uncertainty and ambiguity, it is a journey worth undertaking—a journey that promises not only to expand our scientific horizons but also to deepen our appreciation of the profound beauty and complexity of the universe.

In the quest to decipher the quantum enigma, scientists are continuously pushing the boundaries of knowledge and technology. Experimental innovations, such as quantum teleportation and quantum teleportation, are paving the way for transformative breakthroughs in communication, computation, and cryptography. Quantum teleportation, a process by which the quantum state of one particle is transferred to another instantaneously, holds promise for secure communication networks and quantum internet infrastructure. Quantum computing, with its potential to solve complex problems exponentially faster than classical computers, has the power to revolutionize fields ranging from drug discovery to financial modeling. These advancements underscore the practical implications of quantum mechanics, demonstrating its capacity to transcend theoretical abstraction and catalyze real-world innovation.

The interdisciplinary nature of quantum research fosters collaboration across disparate fields, from physics and chemistry to computer science and engineering. It is a testament to the universality of scientific inquiry, where diverse perspectives converge in pursuit of a shared understanding of the quantum realm. This collaborative ethos is exemplified in initiatives such as the Quantum Flagship program in Europe and the National Quantum Initiative in the United States, which aim to accelerate the development of quantum technologies through strategic investment and interdisciplinary collaboration.

Nevertheless, the quantum revolution is not without its difficulties, despite all of its potential and promise. DE coherence and noise are two technical challenges that pose a serious threat to the stability and dependability of quantum systems, making them impractical for use in real-world applications. Ethical considerations surrounding quantum computing, such as the potential for cryptographic disruption and algorithmic bias, raise complex questions about the societal implications of quantum advancements.

The allure of the quantum frontier persists, drawing researchers and enthusiasts alike into its embrace. It is a realm of infinite possibility, where the laws of classical physics yield to the whims of quantum probability, and the boundaries of reality blur into obscurity. In embracing the uncertainty and embracing the unknown, we embark on a voyage of discovery that transcends the confines of space and time—a journey into the very essence of existence itself. And though the road ahead may be fraught with challenges and uncertainties, it is a road worth traveling, for it promises not only to redefine our understanding of the universe but also to illuminate the path to a future limited only by the bounds of our imagination.

Chapter 7 - Beyond Probability: Statistics and Synchronistic Patterns

Have you ever experienced a moment in life that seemed to defy the laws of probability? Perhaps you met someone who shared an uncanny number of similarities with you, or you stumbled upon a series of events that appeared to be connected by more than mere chance. These instances of synchronicity often leave us questioning the boundaries of statistical probability and pondering the existence of deeper patterns at play in the universe.

Synchronistic events, as coined by Swiss psychiatrist Carl Jung, refer to meaningful coincidences that cannot be explained by conventional notions of cause and effect. While the concept of synchronicity delves into the realm of psychology and spirituality, exploring the interconnectedness of events on a metaphysical level, it also invites us to consider the role of statistics in understanding these phenomena.

Statistics, as a branch of mathematics concerned with the analysis and interpretation of data, offers a framework for quantifying and analyzing patterns in the world around us. From calculating probabilities to identifying correlations, statistics provides a toolset for making sense of complex phenomena, including synchronicity.

At first glance, synchronistic events may appear to be random occurrences with no discernible pattern or explanation. Upon closer examination through the lens of statistics, patterns and correlations may begin to emerge, shedding light on the underlying structure of synchronicity.

One approach to exploring synchronistic patterns through statistics is through the analysis of coincidence frequencies. By collecting data on synchronistic events and quantifying their occurrence over time, researchers can identify whether these events occur more frequently than would be expected by random chance alone.

For example, imagine a study where participants are asked to record instances of synchronicity in their daily lives over the course of several months. Through statistical analysis, researchers can determine whether certain types of synchronistic events occur with greater frequency than expected based on random chance alone. If significant deviations from expected frequencies are observed, it may suggest the presence of underlying patterns or influences at work.

Another statistical approach to studying synchronistic patterns involves correlation analysis. By examining the relationship between different variables associated with synchronistic events, such as time, location, or emotional state, researchers can identify whether these variables are statistically correlated with one another.

For instance, researchers may investigate whether synchronistic events tend to occur more frequently during periods of heightened emotional intensity or whether certain geographic locations are associated with a higher incidence of synchronicity. Through statistical methods such as correlation coefficients and regression analysis, researchers can assess the strength and significance of these relationships, providing insights into the underlying dynamics of synchronistic phenomena.

It's essential to approach the statistical analysis of synchronicity with caution and humility. While statistics can reveal patterns and correlations in data, it cannot capture the full depth and complexity of synchronistic experiences. Synchronicity, by its very nature, transcends conventional explanations and operates on a level that defies quantification.

The interpretation of statistical findings in the context of synchronicity requires a nuanced understanding of both quantitative methods and qualitative insights. While statistics may provide evidence of patterns or correlations, the meaning and significance of synchronistic events ultimately lie in the subjective experiences and interpretations of individuals.

In essence, the intersection of statistics and synchronicity offers a fascinating frontier for exploration, bridging the realms of science and spirituality in the quest to understand the mysteries of the universe. While statistics may illuminate some aspects of synchronistic phenomena, the true essence of these experiences remains elusive, inviting us to embrace the unknown and ponder the deeper mysteries of existence.

In life, there are moments that defy conventional understanding, moments that challenge our perception of probability and coincidence. These instances, known as synchronicity, were coined by Swiss psychiatrist Carl Jung to describe meaningful coincidences that seem to transcend the laws of cause and effect. Synchronicity straddles the realms of psychology and spirituality, prompting us to question the nature of reality and our place within it.

At its core, synchronicity invites contemplation of deeper patterns and interconnectedness in the universe. While it may seem mystical or inexplicable, there is also a statistical dimension to consider. Statistics, as a tool of analysis, allows us to quantify and explore patterns in the seemingly random occurrences of synchronicity.

It's crucial to approach the statistical analysis of synchronicity with caution. While statistics can offer insights into patterns and correlations, they cannot fully encapsulate the depth and complexity of synchronistic experiences. Synchronicity operates beyond the realm of quantification, defying conventional explanation.

Furthermore, the interpretation of statistical findings must be balanced with qualitative insights and subjective experiences. While statistics may provide evidence of patterns, the true meaning and significance of synchronicity are deeply personal and subjective.

In essence, the intersection of statistics and synchronicity opens up a captivating frontier for exploration. It bridges the realms of science and spirituality, challenging us to embrace the mysteries of existence while striving for a deeper understanding of the universe. While statistics may shed light on some aspects of synchronicity, the essence of these experiences remains elusive, reminding us of the boundless complexity of the human experience.

Life is a tapestry woven with threads of mystery and wonder, where moments occasionally emerge that defy the confines of conventional understanding. These instances, encapsulated in the concept of synchronicity by the pioneering insights of Swiss psychiatrist Carl Jung, beckon us to contemplate the intricate interplay between chance and purpose in the fabric of existence.

Synchronicity, as Jung envisioned it, goes beyond the mere coincidence of events; it embodies the idea of meaningful connections unfettered by the constraints of linear causality.

These occurrences, seemingly orchestrated by some unseen hand, prompt us to question the very foundations of our understanding of reality and the universe.

Yet, amidst the enigma of synchronicity lies a realm that beckons exploration through the lens of statistics. Statistics, as a tool of analysis rooted in the principles of probability and data interpretation, offers a gateway to unraveling the underlying patterns within synchronistic phenomena.

The journey into the statistical exploration of synchronicity begins with the recognition that these events, though imbued with a sense of otherworldly significance, are not exempt from the laws governing the distribution of probability. By harnessing the power of statistical methodologies, researchers endeavor to discern the subtle threads that weave synchronistic occurrences into the fabric of our lives.

One avenue of inquiry lies in coincidence frequency analysis, where researchers meticulously document and quantify instances of synchronicity over time. Through rigorous data collection and statistical analysis, they seek to ascertain whether these occurrences exhibit a frequency that exceeds what would be expected by chance alone.

Consider, for instance, a study where participants meticulously record instances of synchronicity in their daily lives over an extended period. Through meticulous analysis, researchers scrutinize the data for deviations from expected probabilities, hinting at the presence of underlying patterns or influences guiding these synchronistic encounters.

Furthermore, correlation analysis emerges as a potent tool in the arsenal of statistical exploration. By scrutinizing the relationship between various variables associated with synchronistic events—be it temporal factors, geographic locations, or emotional states—researchers aim to unveil the intricate web of connections that underpin these seemingly serendipitous occurrences.

For example, researchers might delve into whether synchronistic events tend to cluster during periods of heightened emotional intensity or if certain geographical regions serve as hotspots for these occurrences. Through sophisticated statistical techniques such as correlation coefficients and regression analysis, they endeavor to tease apart the subtle interplay between these variables, offering insights into the underlying dynamics of synchronicity.

Amidst the quest for statistical understanding, it is paramount to tread with humility and reverence for the ineffable nature of synchronicity. While statistics may unveil patterns and correlations within the data, they can only scratch the surface of the profound depth and complexity of these experiences.

The interpretation of statistical findings must be complemented by a nuanced appreciation of qualitative insights and subjective experiences. While statistics may quantify the prevalence of synchronistic events, the true essence and significance of these occurrences reside within the realm of individual interpretation and personal meaning.

In essence, the convergence of statistics and synchronicity heralds a captivating frontier for exploration—one that transcends the boundaries of empirical inquiry and delves into the realms of metaphysical wonder. While statistics may illuminate some facets of synchronistic phenomena, they ultimately serve as signposts guiding us toward a deeper understanding of the mysteries that permeate our existence. Through this synthesis of science and spirituality, we are beckoned to embrace the enigmatic dance of synchronicity, ever mindful of the profound mysteries that lie beyond the grasp of statistical analysis.

Life unfolds as a grand tapestry, interwoven with threads of mystery and wonder, where moments of profound significance occasionally emerge, seemingly defying the constraints of conventional understanding. These instances, encapsulated within the concept of synchronicity by the visionary insights of Swiss psychiatrist Carl Jung, beckon us to embark on a journey of contemplation, exploring the intricate interplay between chance and purpose in the intricate fabric of existence.

Synchronicity, in its essence, transcends the mere happenstance of coincidental events; it embodies the notion of meaningful connections that transcend linear causality, hinting at a deeper order underlying the chaos of existence. These synchronistic encounters, imbued with a sense of profound significance, serve as glimpses into the underlying harmony of the cosmos, inviting us to question the very nature of reality and our place within it.

Yet, within the enigmatic realm of synchronicity lies a frontier awaiting exploration through the lens of statistics. Statistics, as a venerable tool of analysis grounded in the principles of probability and data interpretation, offers a pathway to unraveling the subtle patterns and correlations hidden within synchronistic phenomena.

The odyssey into the statistical exploration of synchronicity commences with the acknowledgment that these events, while imbued with a sense of transcendence, are not exempt from the laws governing the distribution of probability. Through the meticulous application of statistical methodologies, researchers endeavor to discern the subtle threads that weave synchronistic occurrences into the rich tapestry of human experience.

This synthesis of scientific inquiry and spiritual introspection offers a profound opportunity to deepen our understanding of the mysteries that pervade our existence. As we delve further into the exploration of synchronicity through the lens of statistics, we encounter a kaleidoscope of questions and possibilities, each unveiling a new facet of the enigmatic phenomenon.

Beyond the realm of coincidence frequency analysis and correlation studies, lies a vast landscape of statistical methodologies waiting to be harnessed in the pursuit of unraveling the intricacies of synchronicity. Bayesian analysis, for instance, provides a powerful framework for updating our beliefs in light of new evidence, allowing us to refine our understanding of the underlying patterns that govern synchronistic occurrences.

In the Bayesian paradigm, prior beliefs about the nature of synchronicity are combined with observed data to compute the probability of various hypotheses. Through iterative cycles of updating and refinement, researchers can gradually refine their models, shedding light on the underlying mechanisms that give rise to synchronistic phenomena.

The advent of computational methods, such as machine learning and network analysis, opens up exciting avenues for exploring synchronicity on a broader scale. Machine learning algorithms, trained on vast datasets of synchronistic events, can uncover hidden patterns and associations that elude traditional statistical approaches, offering fresh insights into the nature of synchronicity.

Network analysis provides a powerful framework for mapping the intricate web of connections between different variables associated with synchronistic events. By visualizing these networks, researchers can identify central nodes and clusters, revealing the underlying structure of synchronistic phenomena and shedding light on the mechanisms that drive their occurrence.

Yet, amidst the tantalizing array of statistical techniques at our disposal, we must remain cognizant of the limitations inherent in our quest for understanding. Synchronicity, by its very nature, defies reductionism and resists easy categorization within the confines of statistical analysis. Its essence lies in the realm of the ineffable, transcending the bounds of empirical inquiry and inviting us to embrace the mystery of existence.

In this sense, the convergence of statistics and synchronicity serves not as a means of unraveling the mystery, but rather as a catalyst for deepening our appreciation of the enigmatic nature of reality. It reminds us that while statistical analysis may illuminate certain aspects of synchronistic phenomena, the true essence of these experiences lies beyond the reach of empirical observation, residing instead in the realm of personal insight and spiritual awakening.

As we journey onward in our exploration of synchronicity, let us embrace the uncertainty and ambiguity that accompany the quest for understanding. Let us recognize that in the dance between science and spirituality, there are no easy answers or definitive conclusions, only the continual unfolding of mystery and wonder. And let us remain ever mindful of the profound beauty that lies at the intersection of statistics and synchronicity, beckoning us to explore the depths of our shared humanity and the boundless mysteries of the cosmos.

Chapter 8 - Symbolism and Interpretation: Unraveling the Meaning Behind Coincidences

Have you ever experienced a moment where a coincidence seemed too uncanny to be merely chance? Perhaps you bumped into an old friend in a foreign city or stumbled upon a book that contained exactly the answers you were seeking. These instances of synchronicity often leave us pondering the deeper meaning behind them. In the realm of psychology and spirituality, the concept of synchronicity proposes that these seemingly random events are not random at all but rather meaningful coincidences orchestrated by some higher force or cosmic intelligence.

At the heart of synchronicity lies symbolism and interpretation. Every event, encounter, or experience carries symbolic significance that goes beyond its surface appearance. It's like deciphering a hidden code embedded in the fabric of reality, where each symbol acts as a clue guiding us towards a deeper understanding of ourselves and the world around us.

Carl Jung, the renowned Swiss psychiatrist and psychoanalyst, introduced the concept of synchronicity to the world in the early 20th century. He believed that synchronistic events serve as manifestations of the collective unconscious, representing the interconnectedness of all things in the universe. For Jung, these meaningful coincidences were not to be dismissed as mere chance occurrences but rather as glimpses into a profound underlying order.

Understanding the meaning behind coincidences involves a process of interpretation that transcends rationality and logic. It requires us to tap into our intuition and delve into the realm of symbolism, where the language of the unconscious speaks through signs and symbols. Each coincidence becomes a puzzle waiting to be solved, with layers of meaning waiting to be uncovered.

But how do we interpret synchronistic events? There is no one-size-fits-all answer, as the meaning behind each coincidence is deeply personal and subjective. There are some universal principles that can guide us in our interpretation journey.

One approach is to pay attention to recurring themes or patterns in synchronistic events. Do certain symbols or motifs keep appearing in your life? These repetitions could be signaling something significant about your inner psyche or your external circumstances. By keeping a journal and documenting your experiences, you may start to notice recurring symbols that offer valuable insights into your subconscious mind.

Another aspect to consider is the context in which synchronistic events occur. What was happening in your life leading up to the coincidence? What emotions were you experiencing at the time? Sometimes, the meaning behind a coincidence becomes clearer when we reflect on the larger context of our lives and the lessons we are meant to learn.

It's essential to cultivate a sense of openness and receptivity to synchronicity. Being too skeptical or closed-minded can block us from recognizing the deeper meaning behind these events. Instead, approach synchronicity with curiosity and wonder, allowing yourself to be guided by intuition rather than intellect.

In unraveling the meaning behind coincidences, it's crucial to remember that there are no right or wrong interpretations. What matters most is the personal significance that these synchronistic events hold for you. Whether they serve as signs of guidance, affirmation, or reassurance, synchronicity invites us to embrace the mystery and magic of life, knowing that there is a deeper order at work beyond our comprehension.

Have you ever found yourself in a moment where a coincidence seemed too remarkable to chalk up to mere chance? Perhaps it was running into an old friend in a distant city or stumbling upon a book that seemed to hold the answers you've been seeking. These instances of synchronicity often leave us questioning the underlying significance behind them. In the realms of both psychology and spirituality, the notion of synchronicity proposes that these seemingly random occurrences are anything but random; rather, they are purposeful coincidences orchestrated by a higher force or cosmic intelligence.

Symbolism and interpretation lie at the core of synchronicity. Each event, encounter, or experience carries symbolic weight that extends beyond its superficial appearance. It's akin to deciphering a concealed code woven into the fabric of reality, where each symbol serves as a clue guiding us toward deeper self-awareness and comprehension of the world.

Interpreting the meaning behind coincidences necessitates a journey beyond rationality and logic, delving into the realm of intuition and symbolism. It entails unraveling the language of the unconscious, where signs and symbols convey profound messages waiting to be deciphered.

In deciphering the meaning behind coincidences, it's essential to recognize the absence of right or wrong interpretations. The personal significance these synchronistic events hold is paramount. Whether serving as guidance, affirmation, or reassurance, synchronicity encourages an embrace of life's mystery, acknowledging a deeper order at work beyond human comprehension.

The exploration of synchronicity extends beyond mere interpretation into the realm of integration and application. Once we've unraveled the symbolic significance of synchronistic events, the next step is to incorporate these insights into our daily lives. This integration process involves embodying the lessons gleaned from synchronicity and allowing them to inform our actions, decisions, and perceptions of the world around us.

Carl Jung emphasized the transformative potential of synchronicity, viewing it as a catalyst for individuation—the process of becoming whole and integrated individuals. By embracing the messages conveyed through synchronistic events, we embark on a journey of self-discovery and personal growth, aligning ourselves more closely with our authentic selves.

One way to integrate synchronicity into our lives is through mindful reflection and contemplation. Taking the time to reflect on the deeper meaning behind synchronistic encounters allows us to internalize their lessons and insights. Journaling, meditation, and artistic expression are powerful tools for processing and integrating synchronistic experiences into our psyche.

Furthermore, cultivating a sense of gratitude and appreciation for synchronicity enhances our receptivity to future occurrences. By acknowledging and honoring the synchronicities that grace our lives, we create space for more meaningful connections and experiences to unfold. Gratitude serves as a magnet for synchronicity, inviting further moments of alignment and connection.

Additionally, fostering a sense of synchronistic living involves cultivating trust in the inherent wisdom of the universe. Rather than viewing life as a series of random events, we adopt a mindset of cosmic alignment, recognizing that everything unfolds in perfect timing and accordance with a higher plan. Trusting in this divine orchestration allows us to surrender control and embrace the flow of life with grace and ease.

Practicing synchronistic living also entails embracing the interconnectedness of all things. Just as synchronicity reveals the underlying unity of seemingly disparate events, so too does it remind us of our interconnectedness with the world around us. By cultivating compassion, empathy, and a sense of interconnectedness, we deepen our appreciation for the web of life and our place within it.

Integrating synchronicity into our lives involves taking inspired action in alignment with the insights gleaned from these meaningful coincidences. Rather than passively observing synchronistic events, we actively engage with them, allowing them to guide our choices and actions. This may involve following intuitive nudges, pursuing opportunities that present themselves, or making decisions in alignment with our inner guidance.

The journey of synchronicity is a deeply personal and transformative one. As we embrace the messages conveyed through synchronistic events and integrate them into our lives, we align ourselves more closely with the flow of the universe and our true purpose. In doing so, we awaken to the magic and mystery inherent in every moment, living each day with a sense of wonder, purpose, and connection.

Furthermore, the exploration of synchronicity extends beyond the individual level to encompass broader implications for society and the collective consciousness. As synchronistic experiences are inherently interconnected with the fabric of existence, their significance transcends personal narratives to resonate on a societal and even global scale.

At the societal level, recognizing and honoring synchronicity can foster a greater sense of unity and interconnectedness among diverse communities. By acknowledging the meaningful coincidences that weave through our collective experience, we cultivate a shared understanding of the underlying harmony that binds us together. This recognition of synchronicity can serve as a catalyst for social cohesion, empathy, and collaboration, fostering a more harmonious and compassionate society.

Synchronicity has the potential to inspire transformative change and innovation on a global scale. When individuals and organizations attune themselves to the subtle synchronistic cues present in the world around them, they open themselves to new possibilities and opportunities for positive change. Synchronicity can serve as a guiding force, leading humanity toward solutions to complex global challenges, from environmental sustainability to social justice.

Besides, the acknowledgment of synchronicity in the collective consciousness can have profound implications for the way we perceive and interact with the natural world. By recognizing the interconnectedness of all living beings and the intricate web of relationships that sustain life on Earth, we cultivate a deeper reverence for the planet and a greater sense of responsibility toward its preservation. Synchronicity can inspire a shift toward more sustainable and regenerative ways of living, guided by a profound sense of interconnectedness with the natural world.

Furthermore, the recognition of synchronicity in the collective consciousness can facilitate the evolution of human spirituality and consciousness. As individuals awaken to the deeper meaning behind synchronistic experiences, they may undergo profound spiritual transformations, leading to a greater sense of connection with the divine and a deeper understanding of their place within the cosmos. This spiritual awakening can ripple outward, catalyzing a broader shift toward a more compassionate, inclusive, and spiritually awakened society.

The exploration of synchronicity at the societal and collective levels holds the potential to catalyze profound shifts in consciousness and usher in a new era of unity, compassion, and harmony on a global scale. By honoring and integrating synchronicity into our collective awareness, we can cultivate a deeper sense of connection with one another, the natural world, and the cosmos at large, paving the way for a more enlightened and harmonious future for humanity.

The integration of synchronicity into societal structures and systems can lead to transformative shifts in governance, economics, and education. By recognizing the interconnectedness of all individuals and institutions, societies can move toward more inclusive and equitable models that prioritize the well-being of all members. Synchronicity invites us to reconsider traditional hierarchies and power dynamics, fostering a more collaborative and participatory approach to decision-making and governance.

In the realm of economics, embracing synchronicity can inspire the development of sustainable and regenerative models that honor the interconnectedness of economic systems with the natural world. Rather than pursuing endless growth and consumption, societies can adopt principles of sufficiency, balance, and reciprocity, guided by an awareness of the synchronistic relationships that underpin economic transactions. This shift toward a more holistic and interconnected economic paradigm can lead to greater resilience, equity, and harmony within communities and ecosystems.

Synchronicity holds profound implications for the field of education, inviting educators to move beyond traditional approaches focused solely on academic achievement and standardized testing. By integrating the principles of synchronicity into educational curricula, schools can nurture students' innate curiosity, creativity, and intuition, fostering a deeper connection with themselves, others, and the world around them. Synchronicity-based education emphasizes experiential learning, interdisciplinary exploration, and the cultivation of emotional intelligence and empathy, preparing students to navigate an increasingly complex and interconnected world with wisdom and compassion.

Furthermore, the recognition of synchronicity in societal structures and systems can inspire innovative approaches to conflict resolution and peacebuilding. By acknowledging the interconnectedness of all individuals and communities, societies can move away from adversarial and win-lose approaches toward collaborative and win-win solutions that honor the dignity and humanity of all parties involved. Synchronicity-based approaches to conflict resolution emphasize dialogue, empathy, and understanding, seeking to address underlying causes of conflict and promote healing and reconciliation.

In the realm of healthcare, synchronicity offers insights into the interconnectedness of mind, body, and spirit, encouraging a more holistic and integrative approach to healing and wellness. By recognizing the role of synchronicity in the manifestation of illness and the healing process, healthcare practitioners can move beyond purely biomedical models toward more patient-centered and integrative approaches that address the physical, emotional, and spiritual dimensions of health. Synchronicity-based healthcare emphasizes the importance of listening to patients' stories, honoring their unique experiences, and empowering them to play an active role in their own healing journey.

The integration of synchronicity into societal structures and systems offers a pathway toward a more harmonious, compassionate, and sustainable world. By honoring the interconnectedness of all beings and the synchronistic relationships that underpin existence, societies can move toward greater equity, resilience, and flourishing for all members. Synchronicity invites us to recognize the profound interconnectedness of all life and to work together in service of a more just, compassionate, and enlightened future for humanity and the planet.

Chapter 9 - The Role of Intuition: Navigating Synchronistic Events

Intuition, often described as the inner voice or gut feeling, plays a pivotal role in navigating the intricacies of synchronistic events. While rationality and logic have their place in understanding the world, there are certain phenomena, such as synchronicity, that defy conventional explanation and require a different mode of perception.

At its core, intuition is the ability to grasp truths beyond the realm of conscious reasoning. It's like having a sixth sense that allows us to perceive subtle energies and connections that elude the grasp of the rational mind. When it comes to synchronistic events, intuition acts as our compass, guiding us through the labyrinth of meaningful coincidences and helping us decipher their hidden messages.

Unlike analytical thinking, which relies on linear reasoning and empirical evidence, intuition operates on a deeper level of consciousness, where insights arise spontaneously and without conscious effort. It's the voice that whispers in our ear, nudging us towards the right path or warning us of potential dangers ahead. In the realm of synchronicity, intuition serves as our primary tool for discerning the significance behind seemingly random events.

Carl Jung recognized the importance of intuition in the interpretation of synchronistic events. He believed that intuition was the bridge between the conscious and unconscious mind, allowing us to access the symbolic language of the collective unconscious. In moments of synchronicity, our intuition becomes heightened, enabling us to recognize patterns and connections that may not be immediately apparent to the rational mind.

But how do we develop and cultivate our intuition to better navigate synchronistic events? Like any skill, intuition can be honed through practice and self-awareness. One way to strengthen your intuition is to cultivate mindfulness and present moment awareness. By quieting the chatter of the mind and tuning into the subtle sensations of the body, you can create space for intuition to arise naturally.

Another important aspect of intuition is learning to trust your instincts and inner guidance. Often, we dismiss our intuitive insights in favor of rational analysis or societal expectations. Learning to trust your gut feelings and inner knowing can lead to a deeper sense of clarity and alignment with your true path.

Engaging in practices such as meditation, journaling, and dream work can help deepen your connection to intuition and enhance your ability to navigate synchronistic events. These practices allow you to tap into the wisdom of your subconscious mind, where intuition resides, and access insights that may not be accessible through conscious thought alone.

In navigating synchronistic events, it's essential to strike a balance between intuition and discernment. While intuition can provide valuable guidance, it's also essential to approach synchronicity with a healthy dose of skepticism and critical thinking. Not every coincidence holds profound meaning, and it's important to discern between random chance and meaningful synchronicity.

The role of intuition in navigating synchronistic events is about cultivating a deeper connection to ourselves and the world around us. By listening to the whispers of our inner guidance and trusting in the unseen forces at work, we can navigate the twists and turns of life with greater clarity, purpose, and alignment.

At its essence, intuition embodies the capacity to grasp truths beyond conscious reasoning, akin to possessing a sixth sense that allows us to perceive subtle energies and connections evading the grasp of logical deduction. In the realm of synchronistic events, intuition acts as our guiding compass, leading us through the maze of meaningful coincidences and aiding us in unraveling their veiled messages.

Unlike analytical thinking, which relies on linear reasoning and tangible evidence, intuition operates on a deeper plane of consciousness, where insights surface spontaneously and effortlessly. It serves as the gentle whisper in our ear, nudging us toward the right direction or cautioning us of impending risks. Within the domain of synchronicity, intuition stands as our primary tool for deciphering the significance underlying seemingly random occurrences.

Carl Jung, a prominent figure in psychology, acknowledged the pivotal role of intuition in interpreting synchronistic events. He posited that intuition acts as the conduit between the conscious and unconscious realms, granting us access to the symbolic language of the collective unconscious. During moments of synchronicity, our intuition becomes heightened, enabling us to discern patterns and connections that elude rational comprehension.

But how can we nurture and refine our intuition to effectively navigate synchronistic events? Like any skill, intuition thrives on practice and self-awareness. Cultivating mindfulness and present moment awareness serves as a foundational step in strengthening our intuition. By quieting the incessant chatter of the mind and attuning ourselves to the subtle sensations of the body, we create a conducive environment for intuition to emerge organically.

Additionally, learning to trust our instincts and inner guidance plays a crucial role in honing intuition. Frequently, we dismiss intuitive insights in favor of logical analysis or societal norms. Yet, embracing our gut feelings and innate knowing can lead to profound clarity and alignment with our authentic path.

In navigating synchronistic events, striking a balance between intuition and discernment proves imperative. While intuition offers invaluable guidance, it's equally vital to approach synchronicity with a measure of skepticism and critical thinking. Not every coincidence holds profound significance, and discerning between random chance and meaningful synchronicity is paramount.

This deep connection to intuition fosters a profound sense of alignment with the universe and empowers us to navigate the intricate dance of synchronistic events with grace and insight. As we continue to cultivate this connection, we find ourselves attuned to the subtle rhythms of life, effortlessly recognizing the signs and symbols that guide us along our path.

Embracing intuition in navigating synchronistic events opens us to a world of limitless possibilities and opportunities. It allows us to tap into the interconnectedness of all things, recognizing that every encounter, every coincidence, carries with it a deeper meaning and purpose. Through intuition, we come to understand that we are not merely passive observers in the unfolding drama of life but active participants, co-creators of our reality.

Indeed, intuition serves as a beacon of light in times of uncertainty, illuminating the way forward with clarity and wisdom. It grants us the courage to follow our hearts, even when the path ahead seems shrouded in darkness. In embracing intuition, we learn to trust in the inherent wisdom of the universe, knowing that we are always guided and supported, even in the face of adversity.

Furthermore, the cultivation of intuition fosters a deep sense of interconnectedness with all beings. As we attune ourselves to the subtle energies that permeate the fabric of existence, we begin to recognize the inherent oneness that unites us all. Through intuition, we come to understand that we are not separate, isolated entities but interconnected threads in the tapestry of life, each playing a vital role in the grand symphony of existence.

In essence, intuition serves as a bridge between the seen and the unseen, the known and the unknown. It invites us to embrace the mysteries of life with open arms, knowing that within the depths of our intuition lies the key to unlocking the secrets of the universe. As we continue to cultivate and trust in our intuition, we embark on a journey of self-discovery and transformation, unlocking our true potential and aligning ourselves with the infinite possibilities that abound.

Intuition stands as a guiding light in navigating synchronistic events, offering us insight, clarity, and wisdom as we traverse the ever-unfolding landscape of life. Through the cultivation of intuition, we come to understand that synchronicity is not merely a series of random occurrences but a deeply meaningful and interconnected web of experiences that guide us along our path of self-discovery and evolution. As we learn to trust in our intuition and embrace the mysteries of synchronicity, we open ourselves to a world of infinite possibilities and potential, knowing that we are always guided and supported by the unseen forces that shape our reality.

This profound connection to intuition transcends the confines of individual perception, extending its reach to encompass the collective consciousness of humanity. As we embrace our intuitive abilities, we contribute to the collective awakening of consciousness, ushering in a new era of understanding and unity. Through the lens of intuition, we recognize the interconnectedness of all beings and the inherent wisdom that flows through the tapestry of existence.

Intuition serves as a powerful tool for transformation and growth on both personal and collective levels. By attuning ourselves to the subtle whispers of our inner guidance, we gain insight into our deepest desires, fears, and aspirations, unlocking the door to profound self-discovery and self-realization. In embracing intuition, we embark on a journey of healing and empowerment, reclaiming our innate power and sovereignty as co-creators of our reality.

Furthermore, the cultivation of intuition fosters a deep sense of reverence and awe for the mysteries of existence. As we surrender to the guidance of our intuition, we come to realize that life is not meant to be understood or dissected but experienced and embraced with an open heart and mind. Through intuition, we learn to dance with the ebb and flow of life, surrendering to the rhythm of the universe with grace and humility.

Besides, intuition serves as a catalyst for innovation and creativity, inspiring us to think outside the confines of conventional wisdom and explore new realms of possibility. By trusting in the wisdom of our intuition, we break free from the limitations of linear thinking and tap into the boundless wellspring of creativity that lies within us. In doing so, we unleash our creative potential and contribute to the evolution of consciousness in ways we never thought possible.

The cultivation of intuition is a journey of surrender and trust, inviting us to relinquish our attachments to the known and embrace the vast unknown with open arms. As we surrender to the guidance of our intuition, we discover that we are not alone on this journey but supported by the infinite wisdom and love of the universe. Through intuition, we come to realize that we are not separate from the universe but integral parts of its ever-unfolding tapestry, each contributing our unique gifts and talents to the greater whole.

Intuition is a sacred gift that resides within each and every one of us, waiting to be awakened and embraced. As we learn to trust in the wisdom of our intuition, we unlock the door to infinite possibilities and potential, aligning ourselves with the greater purpose and meaning of life. In embracing our intuitive abilities, we embark on a journey of self-discovery and transformation, reclaiming our power and sovereignty as conscious co-creators of our reality.

Furthermore, as we delve deeper into the realms of intuition, we realize its capacity to transcend the boundaries of time and space. Intuition grants us access to a higher dimension of awareness, where past, present, and future converge into a seamless tapestry of existence. Through intuition, we become attuned to the subtle currents of energy that flow through the universe, tapping into the infinite reservoir of wisdom that spans across the ages.

The cultivation of intuition fosters a deep sense of interconnectedness with the natural world. As we attune ourselves to the rhythms of nature, we come to recognize that we are not separate from the Earth but intimately connected to its cycles and seasons. Through intuition, we develop a profound reverence for the sanctity of all life, honoring the interconnected web of existence that sustains us all.

Additionally, intuition serves as a potent tool for navigating the complexities of relationships and interpersonal dynamics. By tuning into the subtle nuances of energy and emotion, we gain insight into the thoughts, feelings, and intentions of others, fostering deeper connections and understanding. Through intuition, we cultivate empathy and compassion, recognizing the inherent divinity within each and every being we encounter.

Furthermore, the cultivation of intuition empowers us to embrace uncertainty and embrace the unknown with courage and resilience. In a world characterized by constant change and upheaval, intuition serves as our guiding light, illuminating the path forward amidst the darkness of uncertainty. Through intuition, we learn to trust in the inherent wisdom of the universe, knowing that we are always supported and guided on our journey.

Intuition serves as a potent catalyst for social and planetary transformation. As we awaken to the wisdom of our intuition, we become agents of change, working towards the creation of a more just, harmonious, and sustainable world. Through intuition, we recognize our interconnectedness with all of humanity and the Earth, inspiring us to take action in service of the greater good.

In essence, intuition is a sacred gift that holds the power to transform our lives and the world around us. As we embrace the wisdom of our intuition, we unlock the door to infinite possibilities and potential, aligning ourselves with the greater purpose and meaning of existence. Through intuition, we come to realize that we are not mere spectators in the unfolding drama of life but active participants, co-creators of our reality.

Chapter 10 - Synchronicity in Dreams: Messages from the Unconscious

Dreams have long been regarded as windows into the subconscious mind, offering insights into our deepest fears, desires, and aspirations. But beyond mere psychological phenomena, dreams also hold the potential for synchronicity, where the boundaries between the inner and outer worlds blur, and meaningful coincidences abound.

Synchronicity in dreams occurs when the symbols, themes, or events portrayed in the dream resonate with events unfolding in waking life. It's like a cosmic dance between the conscious and unconscious realms, where the language of symbolism bridges the gap between inner and outer realities.

Carl Jung, a pioneer in the field of psychology, explored the phenomenon of synchronicity in dreams extensively throughout his career. He believed that dreams were not just random mental chatter but rather meaningful messages from the unconscious, reflecting the deeper currents of the psyche and the collective unconscious.

According to Jung, synchronistic dreams often contain archetypal symbols and motifs that hold universal significance across cultures and time periods. These symbols act as a symbolic language through which the unconscious communicates with the conscious mind, offering guidance, insight, and healing.

Dreams, those enigmatic portals to our subconscious, have fascinated humanity for centuries. They are not mere whimsical fantasies that play out in the theater of our minds while we sleep; rather, they are profound reflections of our innermost fears, desires, and aspirations. Yet, beyond their psychological significance, dreams possess a deeper dimension - one where the threads of our inner world intertwine with the fabric of reality itself, giving rise to the phenomenon known as synchronicity.

Synchronicity, as Carl Jung famously described it, is the occurrence of meaningful coincidences that defy conventional notions of cause and effect. It is the mysterious alignment of events in the external world with the symbols and themes that populate our dreamscape. In essence, it is a harmonious convergence between the conscious and unconscious realms, where the boundaries between inner and outer dissolve into a seamless tapestry of existence.

Jung, the trailblazing psychologist who delved into the depths of the human psyche, devoted much of his career to unraveling the mysteries of synchronicity in dreams. He posited that dreams were not merely the byproduct of random neural activity but rather a form of communication from the unconscious mind, laden with profound meaning and insight.

Central to Jung's theory of synchronicity was the notion of archetypes - universal symbols and motifs that recur across cultures and civilizations. These archetypes, he believed, served as the language of the unconscious, speaking to us through the imagery and narratives of our dreams. Whether it be the wise old sage, the fearsome dragon, or the heroic journey, these archetypal motifs carry a timeless resonance that transcends individual experience.

In synchronistic dreams, these archetypal symbols often take center stage, weaving a narrative that resonates with the events unfolding in our waking lives. It is as if the unconscious mind, attuned to the rhythms of the universe, seeks to impart wisdom and guidance through the language of symbolism. Thus, dreams become not only a reflection of our inner landscape but also a mirror held up to the world around us.

Indeed, the phenomenon of synchronicity challenges our conventional understanding of reality, suggesting that there is a deeper order at play beyond the confines of linear causality. It invites us to contemplate the interconnectedness of all things and the subtle ways in which the universe communicates with us through signs and symbols.

Synchronistic dreams hold profound therapeutic potential, offering a pathway to self-discovery and healing. By exploring the symbolic language of our dreams, we can gain insights into unresolved conflicts, hidden desires, and unconscious patterns that shape our lives. In doing so, we embark on a journey of integration and transformation, reclaiming lost parts of ourselves and forging a deeper connection to the world around us.

In essence, synchronicity in dreams invites us to embrace the mystery of existence and to recognize the profound interconnectedness of all things. It challenges us to look beyond the surface of reality and to listen to the whispers of our inner wisdom. For in the dance of synchronicity, we may find not only meaning and purpose but also a profound sense of unity with the cosmos.

As we delve deeper into the realm of synchronicity, we uncover its intricate tapestry woven not only in dreams but also in the fabric of our everyday lives. The synchronistic principle asserts that meaningful coincidences are not mere chance occurrences but rather reflections of a hidden order that permeates the cosmos. It suggests that there is a subtle interplay between the inner and outer worlds, where our thoughts, emotions, and intentions shape the events that unfold around us.

In the context of dreams, synchronicity manifests in myriad ways, often revealing itself through subtle connections and serendipitous encounters. It is the dream of a long-lost friend preceding their unexpected appearance in our waking life. It is the recurring motif of a key symbolizing unlocking new opportunities just as we find ourselves at a crossroads. These synchronistic moments serve as signposts on our journey of self-discovery, guiding us towards greater awareness and fulfillment.

The study of synchronicity extends beyond the individual psyche to encompass collective phenomena that defy rational explanation. Throughout history, there have been countless accounts of synchronistic events occurring on a grand scale, from simultaneous discoveries in science and technology to the collective dreams and visions that shape cultural movements and revolutions. These synchronicities hint at a deeper order that binds humanity together in a web of interconnectedness, transcending the boundaries of time and space.

One of the most intriguing aspects of synchronicity is its role in facilitating meaningful connections between individuals. It is the uncanny sense of familiarity we feel upon meeting a stranger for the first time, as if we have known them in another lifetime. It is the shared dreams and telepathic experiences that bridge the gap between minds separated by distance and time. In this way, synchronicity serves as a catalyst for the formation of meaningful relationships and the cultivation of community bonds.

Furthermore, the exploration of synchronicity opens up new vistas of inquiry into the nature of reality itself. It challenges us to reexamine our assumptions about the nature of time, causality, and the limits of human perception. In the quantum realm, where particles can be entangled across vast distances instantaneously, synchronicity finds its echo in the interconnectedness of all things. It suggests that the universe is not a collection of separate, isolated entities but rather a unified whole in which every part is intimately connected to the whole.

In the realm of psychology, synchronicity offers a bridge between the subjective experiences of the individual and the objective observations of the scientific method. While traditional psychology tends to focus on measurable phenomena and empirical data, synchronicity invites us to embrace the richness of subjective experience and the power of intuition and imagination. It encourages us to trust in the wisdom of the unconscious mind and to honor the symbolic language through which it communicates with us.

Synchronicity in dreams is a profound phenomenon that invites us to explore the depths of our own psyche and the mysteries of the universe. It challenges us to look beyond the surface of reality and to recognize the interconnectedness of all things. Whether viewed through the lens of psychology, philosophy, or quantum physics, synchronicity offers a glimpse into the underlying order that shapes our lives and our world. As we continue to unravel its mysteries, we may find ourselves on a journey of discovery that leads us to new insights, new connections, and ultimately, to a deeper understanding of ourselves and the cosmos.

In our exploration of synchronicity, we uncover its subtle nuances and profound implications for our understanding of reality. Beyond the confines of linear time and causality, synchronicity hints at a deeper layer of existence where past, present, and future coalesce into a seamless whole. It challenges us to reevaluate our perceptions of the world and to embrace the interconnectedness of all things.

One of the remarkable aspects of synchronicity is its ability to transcend cultural and linguistic barriers, speaking to the universal truths that bind humanity together. Whether through dreams, visions, or chance encounters, synchronicity reveals the underlying patterns that shape our lives and our collective destiny. It is the thread that weaves through the tapestry of human experience, connecting us to each other and to the cosmic order.

The study of synchronicity opens up new avenues of exploration in fields as diverse as anthropology, mythology, and the arts. Across cultures and civilizations, we find echoes of synchronistic themes and motifs that speak to the timeless truths of the human condition. From the ancient myths and legends that resonate with archetypal symbolism to the modern-day synchronicities that defy rational explanation, we are reminded of the interconnectedness of all things and the power of the human spirit to transcend limitations.

In the realm of personal growth and transformation, synchronicity serves as a catalyst for profound inner change. It is the wake-up call that shakes us out of complacency and propels us towards our highest potential. By paying attention to the synchronicities that occur in our lives, we gain valuable insights into our unconscious desires, fears, and aspirations. We become more attuned to the subtle signals that guide us along our path, trusting in the wisdom of the universe to lead us towards greater fulfillment and purpose.

Furthermore, the study of synchronicity invites us to adopt a more holistic view of reality that embraces both the seen and the unseen, the known and the unknown. It encourages us to cultivate a sense of wonder and awe in the face of life's mysteries, recognizing that there is much more to existence than meets the eye. In doing so, we open ourselves up to new possibilities and perspectives, expanding our consciousness and deepening our connection to the world around us.

Synchronicity in dreams is a multifaceted phenomenon that transcends conventional explanations and invites us to explore the mysteries of existence. It challenges us to expand our understanding of reality and to embrace the interconnectedness of all things. Whether viewed through the lens of psychology, spirituality, or science, synchronicity offers a profound glimpse into the underlying order that governs our lives and our universe. As we continue to delve into its mysteries, we may find ourselves on a journey of discovery that leads us to new insights, new connections, and ultimately, to a deeper sense of meaning and purpose in our lives.

Furthermore, the exploration of synchronicity leads us to reconsider our relationship with time and space. In the tapestry of synchronistic events, past, present, and future converge, suggesting a nonlinear perspective on temporal reality. This challenges our conventional understanding of time as a linear progression and invites us to envision a more expansive, interconnected view of the cosmos. In the realm of synchronicity, every moment is pregnant with possibility, every encounter pregnant with meaning, transcending the limitations of chronological order.

Synchronicity serves as a potent reminder of our interconnectedness with the natural world and the cosmos at large. Just as the moon influences the tides and the stars guide sailors across vast oceans, synchronicity suggests that we are intimately connected to the rhythms and patterns of the universe. It is a call to attunement, urging us to listen to the whispers of the wind, the songs of the birds, and the wisdom of the earth. In doing so, we come to recognize that we are not separate from nature but rather an integral part of its intricate web of life.

In the realm of quantum physics, synchronicity finds resonance in the principle of entanglement, where particles separated by vast distances instantaneously influence each other's states. This phenomenon hints at a deeper level of interconnectedness that transcends the boundaries of space and time, suggesting a fundamental unity underlying all of existence. In this paradigm, synchronicity is not merely a curious anomaly but rather a reflection of the underlying fabric of reality itself, where everything is interconnected in a vast, cosmic dance of energy and information.

Furthermore, the study of synchronicity challenges us to reexamine our notions of causality and free will. While traditional science operates within the framework of cause and effect, synchronicity suggests that there may be other forces at play beyond our understanding. It invites us to embrace the mystery of existence and to acknowledge the limits of our rational faculties in grappling with the complexities of the universe. In doing so, we open ourselves up to a more nuanced understanding of reality, one that embraces the enigmatic and the inexplicable with humility and awe.

Synchronicity in dreams offers a gateway to profound insights and revelations that transcend the boundaries of individual consciousness. It is a reminder of the interconnectedness of all things and the hidden order that underlies the chaos of everyday life. As we continue to explore the mysteries of synchronicity, we may find ourselves on a journey of discovery that leads us to new horizons of understanding and appreciation for the wonders of the universe.

The study of synchronicity encourages us to cultivate a deeper sense of presence and mindfulness in our daily lives. By paying attention to the subtle synchronicities that occur around us, we become more attuned to the rhythms of the universe and the interconnectedness of all things. This heightened awareness allows us to move through life with greater grace and intention, guided by the wisdom of the synchronistic principle.

In the realm of personal growth and transformation, synchronicity serves as a powerful tool for self-discovery and inner healing. By exploring the messages and symbols that arise in our dreams and waking experiences, we gain valuable insights into our unconscious motivations, fears, and desires. This process of introspection and reflection enables us to release old patterns and beliefs that no longer serve us, opening the door to profound healing and transformation.

Furthermore, the study of synchronicity invites us to embrace a more holistic understanding of reality that transcends the limitations of reductionist thinking. Rather than viewing the world as a collection of separate, isolated phenomena, synchronicity encourages us to see the interconnectedness and interdependence of all things. In this interconnected web of existence, every thought, action, and intention ripples outwards, influencing the fabric of reality in subtle yet profound ways.

In the realm of creativity and innovation, synchronicity serves as a source of inspiration and insight. Many artists, scientists, and visionaries throughout history have credited synchronistic experiences with sparking their most groundbreaking ideas and discoveries. By remaining open to the serendipitous connections and unexpected revelations that arise, we tap into a wellspring of creative potential that lies beyond the confines of rational thought.

The exploration of synchronicity invites us to cultivate a sense of wonder and awe in the face of life's mysteries. It reminds us that there is much about the universe that we do not yet understand, and that the journey of discovery is as important as the destination. In embracing the unknown with curiosity and humility, we open ourselves up to new possibilities and perspectives that enrich our lives and expand our horizons.

Synchronicity in dreams and waking life offers us a profound opportunity to deepen our understanding of ourselves and the world around us. It is a reminder of the interconnectedness of all things and the hidden patterns that shape our lives. As we continue to explore the mysteries of synchronicity, we may find ourselves embarking on a journey of self-discovery, creativity, and spiritual awakening that leads us to new heights of understanding and fulfillment.

Chapter 11 - Serendipity in Science: Discoveries and Innovations

Serendipity, often hailed as the fortuitous stroke of luck or chance, has played a profound role in shaping the landscape of scientific discovery and innovation. While meticulous planning and methodical inquiry form the bedrock of scientific progress, serendipitous moments of insight and discovery have frequently emerged from unexpected sources, leading to groundbreaking advances across various fields of study.

One of the most famous examples of serendipity in science is the discovery of penicillin by Alexander Fleming in 1928. While conducting research on bacterial cultures, Fleming noticed that a mold called Penicillium notatum had inadvertently contaminated one of his petri dishes. To his astonishment, he observed that the mold inhibited the growth of bacteria, paving the way for the development of the first antibiotic. Fleming's chance observation revolutionized the field of medicine, saving countless lives and ushering in the era of antibiotics.

The discovery of the microwave oven is another serendipitous tale of scientific ingenuity. In 1945, engineer Percy Spencer was conducting experiments with radar equipment when he noticed that a chocolate bar in his pocket had melted. Intrigued by this unexpected phenomenon, Spencer realized that the microwaves emitted by the radar equipment were responsible for heating the chocolate. This serendipitous observation led to the invention of the microwave oven, revolutionizing the way we cook and prepare food.

In the realm of physics, serendipity has also played a crucial role in the discovery of new phenomena and fundamental principles. The accidental discovery of radioactivity by Henri Becquerel in 1896, for example, occurred when he observed that uranium salts emitted mysterious rays that could expose photographic plates. This serendipitous discovery laid the foundation for our understanding of nuclear physics and the structure of the atom.

Serendipity is not limited to individual discoveries but can also shape the trajectory of entire scientific disciplines. The field of genetics, for instance, owes much to the serendipitous discovery of the structure of DNA by James Watson and Francis Crick in 1953. Their groundbreaking insight into the double-helix structure of DNA, based in part on data collected by Rosalind Franklin, revolutionized our understanding of heredity and laid the groundwork for modern molecular biology.

While serendipity may seem like a stroke of luck or chance, it often stems from a combination of keen observation, creative thinking, and openness to unexpected possibilities. Scientists who embrace serendipity cultivate a mindset of curiosity and exploration, allowing them to recognize and capitalize on unexpected discoveries that arise in the course of their research.

Besides its practical applications in scientific research, serendipity also underscores the inherent unpredictability and complexity of the natural world. While scientists strive to uncover the underlying laws and principles that govern the universe, serendipitous discoveries remind us that nature is full of surprises and mysteries waiting to be uncovered.

Serendipity has long been recognized as a driving force behind scientific discovery and innovation. From the accidental discovery of penicillin to the serendipitous observation of radioactivity, moments of chance and insight have reshaped our understanding of the world and propelled humanity forward. By embracing serendipity, scientists can tap into the creative potential of the unknown, opening new avenues of exploration and discovery that transcend the boundaries of conventional thinking.

Serendipity, often described as the unexpected stroke of luck or chance, has continuously played a pivotal role in the evolution of scientific exploration and innovation. While meticulous planning and systematic investigation are essential components of scientific advancement, it is the serendipitous instances of insight and discovery that have frequently catalyzed groundbreaking progress across diverse fields of study.

While serendipity may be construed as a stroke of luck or chance, its genesis often lies in a blend of acute observation, innovative thinking, and receptivity to unforeseen opportunities. Scientists attuned to serendipity nurture a mindset of curiosity and exploration, enabling them to discern and capitalize on unexpected discoveries that arise during their research endeavors.

Beyond its practical implications in scientific inquiry, serendipity underscores the inherent unpredictability and intricacy of the natural world. While scientists endeavor to unravel the underlying laws and principles governing the cosmos, serendipitous revelations serve as poignant reminders that nature abounds with enigmas and surprises awaiting revelation.

Serendipity emerges as a formidable catalyst propelling scientific discovery and innovation forward. From the happenstance unearthing of penicillin to the serendipitous detection of radioactivity, moments of chance and insight have reshaped humanity's understanding of the world. Embracing serendipity enables scientists to unlock the creative potential of the unknown, charting new frontiers of exploration and discovery that transcend the confines of conventional wisdom.

This embrace of serendipity not only enhances scientific inquiry but also fosters a deeper appreciation for the complexity and richness of the universe. Serendipitous discoveries often challenge prevailing assumptions and paradigms, pushing the boundaries of human knowledge and imagination.

Consider the accidental discovery of the cosmic microwave background radiation (CMB) by Arno Penzias and Robert Wilson in 1964. Initially baffled by mysterious noise interfering with their radio antenna, the duo stumbled upon a signal originating from all directions in the universe. This serendipitous finding provided compelling evidence for the Big Bang theory, fundamentally altering our understanding of the cosmos and the origins of the universe.

Serendipity frequently intersects with interdisciplinary collaborations, fostering unexpected connections and synergies across disparate fields. The serendipitous discovery of graphene, a two-dimensional allotrope of carbon with extraordinary properties, exemplifies this phenomenon. In 2004, Andre Geim and Konstantin Novoselov serendipitously isolated graphene while investigating the properties of carbon-based materials using adhesive tape. This chance discovery paved the way for a plethora of applications, spanning from electronics to materials science and beyond.

Furthermore, serendipity often thrives in environments that encourage risk-taking and experimentation. The culture of innovation prevalent in institutions like Bell Labs in the mid-20th century exemplifies this ethos. Serendipitous discoveries such as the invention of the transistor by John Bardeen, Walter Brattain, and William Shockley in 1947 emerged from a fertile ground of collaborative inquiry and exploration, where researchers were empowered to pursue curiosity-driven investigations.

Beyond the realm of scientific research, serendipity permeates various aspects of human endeavor, including art, literature, and entrepreneurship. The serendipitous encounters and unforeseen opportunities often encountered in creative pursuits underscore the role of chance in shaping cultural evolution and artistic expression.

In literature, authors often draw inspiration from serendipitous moments or chance encounters, weaving them into narratives that captivate and resonate with readers. Entrepreneurs frequently cite serendipity as a driving force behind transformative innovations and business breakthroughs. Chance meetings, fortuitous connections, and unexpected insights can catalyze entrepreneurial endeavors, leading to the birth of disruptive technologies and novel business models.

The digital age has further amplified the role of serendipity in everyday life, as algorithms and recommendation systems strive to anticipate and fulfill our preferences. Yet, amidst the algorithmic curation of content and information, there remains a longing for serendipitous discoveries that defy expectations and broaden our horizons.

In essence, serendipity serves as a potent reminder of the inherent uncertainty and wonder that permeate existence.

While we may strive for control and predictability, serendipitous moments remind us of the beauty and possibility inherent in chance encounters and unexpected revelations.

Embracing serendipity requires a willingness to relinquish rigid expectations and embrace the unknown with an open mind and heart. It beckons us to explore the uncharted territories of possibility, where the intersection of chance and intentionality gives rise to moments of profound insight and discovery.

Serendipity invites us to dance with uncertainty, to embrace the unexpected with curiosity and grace. In doing so, we unlock the boundless potential of the universe, charting a course of exploration and innovation that transcends the confines of our imagination. As we navigate the serendipitous journey of life, let us cherish the moments of chance and wonder that enrich our existence and propel us ever forward into the vast unknown.

Serendipity, with its enigmatic allure, continues to weave its subtle threads through the tapestry of human experience, transcending boundaries and defying expectations. Its influence extends far beyond the realms of science and innovation, permeating every facet of existence with a touch of magic and mystery.

In the realm of social dynamics, serendipity often manifests in the form of unexpected connections and synchronicities that bring people together. Chance encounters at social gatherings, random encounters on the street, or even virtual interactions in online communities can spark meaningful relationships and collaborations that profoundly impact lives. These serendipitous moments serve as reminders of the interconnectedness of humanity and the profound beauty of shared experiences.

Serendipity infuses the creative process with an element of spontaneity and exploration. Artists, musicians, and creators of all kinds often find inspiration in unexpected places, stumbling upon ideas and insights that defy conventional logic. A chance glimpse of a sunset, a fleeting melody heard in passing, or a serendipitous encounter with a stranger can ignite the creative spark, leading to the birth of masterpieces that resonate across generations.

In the world of business and entrepreneurship, serendipity plays a pivotal role in shaping the trajectory of ventures and enterprises. Entrepreneurs who remain open to serendipitous opportunities often find themselves at the nexus of innovation and disruption, leveraging chance encounters and unforeseen circumstances to propel their ventures to new heights. Serendipitous partnerships, strategic alliances, and fortuitous market trends can transform fledgling startups into industry leaders, illustrating the transformative power of chance in the entrepreneurial journey.

Furthermore, serendipity permeates the fabric of cultural evolution, shaping the course of history in ways both subtle and profound. Historical events often unfold in response to a confluence of factors, including chance occurrences and serendipitous encounters that defy rational explanation. From the accidental discovery of continents by explorers to the chance encounters that sparked revolutions, serendipity has left an indelible mark on the annals of human history, shaping the destinies of nations and civilizations.

In the realm of personal growth and self-discovery, serendipity serves as a guiding force, nudging individuals towards paths of fulfillment and purpose. Chance encounters with mentors, unexpected opportunities for growth, and serendipitous moments of clarity can catalyze transformative journeys of self-realization and empowerment. By embracing the serendipitous nature of life, individuals can cultivate a sense of openness and receptivity, allowing them to fully embrace the richness and complexity of the human experience.

Serendipity remains an ever-present force in the tapestry of human existence, weaving its subtle magic through the fabric of life. From the serendipitous discoveries that reshape our understanding of the universe to the chance encounters that shape our personal and professional trajectories, serendipity invites us to embrace the unknown with open hearts and minds. In doing so, we unlock the boundless potential of the universe, charting a course of exploration and discovery that transcends the confines of our imagination. As we navigate the serendipitous journey of life, let us cherish the moments of chance and wonder that enrich our existence and connect us to the infinite possibilities that lie beyond.

Serendipity, the delightful dance of chance and opportunity, continues to unfold its intricate patterns across the canvas of human experience, beckoning us to embrace the unexpected with open arms and curious minds. As we traverse the labyrinth of life, serendipitous moments pepper our journey, infusing each step with a sense of wonder and possibility.

In the realm of education and learning, serendipity serves as a catalyst for intellectual growth and discovery. Students who remain receptive to unexpected connections and insights often find themselves enriched by serendipitous encounters with knowledge and wisdom. A chance conversation with a peer, a random encounter with a thought-provoking book, or a serendipitous discovery in the midst of research can open new vistas of understanding and inspire lifelong curiosity.

Serendipity plays a transformative role in the realm of healthcare and wellness, where chance occurrences can lead to breakthroughs in treatment and care. Medical professionals attuned to the serendipitous nature of healing often find themselves at the forefront of innovation, leveraging unexpected insights and discoveries to improve patient outcomes and advance medical science. Serendipitous encounters with new therapies, unexpected responses to treatment, and chance observations in clinical practice can shape the course of medical research and pave the way for new frontiers in healthcare.

In the realm of environmental conservation and sustainability, serendipity often emerges as a guiding principle, leading to unexpected solutions to pressing ecological challenges. Conservationists and environmental scientists who remain open to serendipitous discoveries often find innovative ways to protect and preserve the natural world. A chance observation of wildlife behavior, a serendipitous discovery of a new species, or an unexpected breakthrough in sustainable technology can inspire novel approaches to conservation and usher in a brighter, more sustainable future for our planet.

Furthermore, serendipity infuses the realm of technology and innovation with an element of excitement and possibility. Inventors and technologists who embrace the serendipitous nature of discovery often find themselves at the forefront of technological breakthroughs. A chance experiment in the lab, a serendipitous encounter with a new material, or an unexpected application of existing technology can lead to groundbreaking innovations that reshape industries and transform society.

In the realm of spirituality and personal growth, serendipity serves as a guiding force, leading individuals towards paths of self-discovery and enlightenment. Those who remain open to the serendipitous unfolding of life often find themselves aligned with their true purpose and destiny. A chance encounter with a spiritual teacher, a serendipitous moment of insight and clarity, or an unexpected twist of fate can catalyze profound spiritual awakenings and transformative journeys of self-realization.

In essence, serendipity invites us to embrace the inherent uncertainty and beauty of life, reminding us that the most extraordinary moments often arise from the most unexpected circumstances. As we navigate the serendipitous journey of existence, let us cultivate a spirit of openness and receptivity, allowing ourselves to be guided by the gentle whispers of chance and possibility. In doing so, we unlock the boundless potential of the universe, charting a course of exploration and discovery that transcends the confines of our imagination.

Chapter 12 - The Power of Storytelling: Mythology and Synchronistic Narratives

Throughout human history, storytelling has served as a powerful tool for transmitting knowledge, preserving cultural traditions, and exploring the mysteries of existence. Across diverse cultures and civilizations, myths and legends have woven tales of gods and heroes, monsters and magic, creating rich tapestries of meaning and symbolism that resonate with the human psyche. Within these timeless narratives lie echoes of synchronicity, the mysterious phenomenon of meaningful coincidences that seem to defy rational explanation.

Mythology abounds with examples of synchronistic narratives, where characters encounter serendipitous events and chance occurrences that shape their destinies. In Greek mythology, for example, the concept of fate, or "moira," played a central role in the lives of mortals and gods alike. Heroes such as Oedipus and Achilles grappled with prophecies and omens that foretold their fates, leading to tragic yet fateful outcomes. These synchronistic elements underscored the interconnectedness of human lives with the larger forces of destiny and divine intervention.

In Norse mythology, the concept of wyrd, or fate, permeated the tales of gods and giants, warriors and seers. The Norns, three mysterious sisters who spun the threads of fate, wove the destinies of gods and mortals alike, shaping the course of events with their unseen hands. Synchronistic events often played a pivotal role in the lives of Norse heroes, guiding them along their paths with signs and omens that hinted at the workings of a larger cosmic order.

Besides to classical mythology, synchronistic narratives are also found in religious texts and spiritual traditions around the world. The Bible, for example, is replete with stories of divine intervention and providential guidance, where seemingly chance events lead to profound moments of revelation and transformation. From the parting of the Red Sea to the conversion of Saul on the road to Damascus, these synchronistic narratives speak to the mysterious ways in which the divine intersects with human affairs.

In more recent times, the power of storytelling to convey synchronistic themes has found expression in literature, film, and other forms of creative expression. Authors such as J.R.R. Tolkien and C.S. Lewis wove tales of epic adventure and cosmic struggle, drawing upon mythic archetypes and synchronistic motifs to captivate readers' imaginations. Filmmakers such as George Lucas and Steven Spielberg have crafted cinematic masterpieces that explore the interplay of fate, destiny, and free will in the lives of their characters.

At its core, storytelling serves as a mirror of the human experience, reflecting our deepest hopes, fears, and aspirations. Through myths and legends, we confront the mysteries of existence and grapple with the complexities of the human condition. Synchronistic narratives, with their themes of chance and destiny, remind us that life is a journey filled with unexpected twists and turns, where meaning can be found in the most unlikely of places.

The power of storytelling to convey synchronistic themes is a testament to the enduring fascination with the mysteries of existence. Whether found in ancient myths or modern literature, synchronistic narratives offer glimpses into the hidden patterns and connections that shape our lives. By embracing the power of storytelling, we can unlock the transformative potential of synchronicity, finding meaning and purpose in the unfolding tapestry of human experience.

Throughout the annals of human history, storytelling has stood as a potent conduit for the transmission of wisdom, the preservation of cultural heritage, and the contemplation of life's enigmatic depths. From the dawn of civilization to the present day, myths and legends have served as the warp and weft of our collective narrative, interlacing tales of divine beings, heroic exploits, and cosmic mysteries that resonate with the soul of humanity. Embedded within these timeless sagas lie echoes of synchronicity, the tantalizing phenomenon of meaningful coincidences that defy the confines of rational explanation.

Beyond the confines of classical mythologies, synchronistic narratives find resonance within the sacred texts and spiritual traditions of diverse cultures and faiths across the globe. In the pages of the Bible, for instance, tales of divine providence and providential intervention abound, where seemingly random events coalesce to catalyze moments of profound revelation and spiritual awakening. From the miraculous parting of the Red Sea to the transformative encounter of Saul on the road to Damascus, these synchronistic vignettes serve as testament to the inscrutable ways in which the divine intercedes in the affairs of mortals.

At its essence, storytelling serves as a mirror reflecting the kaleidoscopic spectrum of the human experience, offering glimpses into the unfathomable depths of our collective psyche. Through the prism of myth and legend, we confront the existential mysteries that lie at the heart of our existence, grappling with questions of identity, purpose, and ultimate meaning. Synchronistic narratives, with their evocative blend of chance and destiny, beckon us to journey beyond the veil of mundane reality, where the mundane and the miraculous converge in a symphony of cosmic significance.

The enduring resonance of synchronistic themes within the realm of storytelling bears testament to our eternal quest for meaning and understanding in a universe fraught with mystery and wonder. Whether found within the hallowed halls of ancient myths or the dazzling vistas of modern imagination, synchronistic narratives serve as guides illuminating the hidden pathways of fate and fortune that thread through the tapestry of human experience. By embracing the transformative power of storytelling, we embark on a voyage of discovery through the labyrinth of synchronicity, unlocking the latent potential for growth, insight, and enlightenment that lies dormant within the recesses of our collective unconscious.

In exploring the expansive terrain of synchronicity within storytelling, it becomes apparent that this phenomenon transcends cultural boundaries and temporal epochs, manifesting in myriad forms across diverse narratives and artistic expressions. Within the intricate weave of Eastern mythology, for instance, tales of karma and destiny intertwine with the threads of synchronicity, weaving a tapestry of interconnectedness and spiritual awakening. In Hindu mythology, the concept of "karma" dictates the cyclical nature of existence, wherein the deeds of past lives shape the destiny of souls in their journey towards enlightenment. Synchronistic events, imbued with the subtle workings of cosmic justice, serve as signposts along the path of self-realization, guiding individuals towards a deeper understanding of their place within the vast web of existence.

Within the rich tapestry of Chinese mythology and folklore, synchronistic themes resonate with the ancient principles of Taoism and Confucianism, offering insights into the interplay of yin and yang, fate and free will. The concept of "Dao," or the Way, permeates Chinese cosmology, guiding individuals along the path of harmonious living in accordance with the rhythms of nature. Synchronistic occurrences, imbued with the subtle wisdom of the Tao, illuminate the hidden pathways of destiny, revealing the interconnectedness of all things in the grand tapestry of existence.

The exploration of synchronicity within indigenous mythologies and oral traditions unveils a rich tapestry of cultural wisdom and ancestral knowledge passed down through generations. In the indigenous traditions of the Americas, for example, stories of animal spirits, nature deities, and sacred ceremonies are imbued with synchronistic significance, serving as guides for harmonious living and spiritual connection with the land. Synchronistic events, such as encounters with spirit animals or visions during rituals, are regarded as messages from the ancestors and the natural world, offering guidance and protection on the journey of life.

In the realm of contemporary literature and popular culture, the allure of synchronistic themes continues to captivate audiences through a diverse array of genres and mediums. From the magical realism of Gabriel García Márquez to the speculative fiction of Philip K. Dick, synchronistic narratives infuse works of literature with an air of mystery and intrigue, inviting readers to ponder the hidden currents of fate that shape the human experience. Likewise, in the realm of film and television, storytellers such as Christopher Nolan and David Lynch have explored the enigmatic nature of synchronicity, weaving intricate narratives that blur the boundaries between reality and illusion, chance and destiny.

At its core, the exploration of synchronicity within storytelling serves as a gateway to deeper realms of insight and understanding, inviting individuals to contemplate the mysterious forces that govern the unfolding drama of life. Through the lens of myth and legend, we glimpse the hidden patterns and connections that underlie the tapestry of existence, revealing the profound interconnectedness of all things in the vast cosmic dance of creation. By embracing the transformative power of synchronistic storytelling, we embark on a journey of discovery through the labyrinth of the human soul, unlocking the latent potential for growth, healing, and spiritual awakening that lies dormant within each of us.

The exploration of synchronicity within storytelling offers a profound opportunity for individuals to delve into the mysteries of existence and awaken to the interconnected web of life that binds us all together. Whether found within ancient myths or contemporary narratives, synchronistic themes serve as guides illuminating the hidden pathways of fate and fortune that shape our journey through the cosmos. By embracing the transformative power of synchronistic storytelling, we embark on a journey of self-discovery and spiritual awakening, unlocking the latent potential for growth, healing, and enlightenment that lies within the recesses of our collective consciousness.

In delving deeper into the realm of synchronicity within storytelling, it becomes evident that this phenomenon not only reflects the intricacies of the human psyche but also mirrors the underlying patterns and rhythms of the cosmos itself. Across cultures and civilizations, from the ancient myths of Mesopotamia to the modern narratives of science fiction, synchronistic themes resonate with a timeless resonance, inviting individuals to contemplate the mysterious interplay of chance and destiny that shapes the unfolding drama of existence.

Within the pantheon of Mesopotamian mythology, for instance, tales of gods and goddesses, demons and heroes, are infused with the subtle currents of synchronicity, reflecting the cosmic dance of creation and destruction that underlies the fabric of reality. In the Epic of Gilgamesh, one of the oldest surviving works of literature, the titular hero embarks on a quest for immortality, only to confront the inevitability of death and the ephemeral nature of human existence. Synchronistic events, such as encounters with divine beings and trials of courage and wisdom, serve as catalysts for Gilgamesh's spiritual transformation, guiding him towards a deeper understanding of the mysteries of life and death.

Within the rich tapestry of African mythology and oral traditions, synchronistic narratives abound with tales of ancestral spirits, nature deities, and mythical creatures that inhabit the liminal spaces between the seen and unseen worlds. In the folklore of the Yoruba people of Nigeria, for example, the Orishas, divine beings imbued with the powers of creation and transformation, shape the destinies of mortals through synchronistic encounters and interventions. Synchronistic events, such as dreams, visions, and divinatory rituals, serve as portals through which individuals can commune with the ancestral spirits and tap into the hidden currents of cosmic wisdom that flow through the universe.

The exploration of synchronicity within contemporary literature and popular culture reveals a kaleidoscopic array of narratives that probe the depths of human consciousness and the mysteries of the cosmos. In the works of authors such as Haruki Murakami and Neil Gaiman, synchronistic themes infuse tales of magical realism and speculative fiction with an air of existential wonder and philosophical inquiry. Through the prism of synchronicity, characters grapple with questions of identity, purpose, and the nature of reality, embarking on transformative journeys of self-discovery and enlightenment.

In the realm of cinema and television, storytellers such as David Fincher and Lana Wachowski have explored the enigmatic nature of synchronicity, weaving intricate narratives that blur the boundaries between the mundane and the miraculous, the rational and the irrational. From the mind-bending twists of "Fight Club" to the existential mysteries of "The Matrix," synchronistic motifs serve as metaphors for the hidden forces that shape our lives and the choices we make along the way.

At its essence, the exploration of synchronicity within storytelling invites individuals to contemplate the interconnected web of life that binds us all together, transcending the limitations of time and space to reveal the underlying unity of creation. Through the medium of myth and legend, we glimpse the hidden patterns and connections that underlie the tapestry of existence, awakening to the profound realization that we are not merely passive observers but active participants in the cosmic drama of life.

The exploration of synchronicity within storytelling offers a profound opportunity for individuals to awaken to the deeper mysteries of existence and tap into the hidden currents of cosmic wisdom that flow through the universe. Whether found within ancient myths or contemporary narratives, synchronistic themes serve as guides illuminating the path of self-discovery and spiritual awakening, inviting us to embark on a journey of exploration and transformation that transcends the confines of ordinary reality. By embracing the transformative power of synchronistic storytelling, we open ourselves to the infinite possibilities of the cosmos, unlocking the latent potential for growth, healing, and enlightenment that lies within each of us.

Chapter 13 - Spiritual Perspectives: Synchronicity in Eastern Philosophy and Religions

In the rich tapestry of Eastern philosophy and religions, the concept of synchronicity finds resonance with ancient wisdom traditions that emphasize the interconnectedness of all things. From Hinduism and Buddhism to Taoism and Confucianism, spiritual perspectives on synchronicity offer profound insights into the nature of reality, consciousness, and the human experience.

In Hinduism, the concept of karma lies at the heart of synchronistic understanding, suggesting that actions have consequences that unfold over time according to the law of cause and effect. Every thought, word, and deed leaves an imprint on the soul, shaping one's destiny in this life and the next.

The intricate fabric of Eastern philosophy and spiritual traditions unveils a profound understanding of synchronicity, an idea deeply ingrained in ancient wisdom teachings that emphasize the interconnectedness of all existence. Across Hinduism, Buddhism, Taoism, and Confucianism, synchronicity is woven into the tapestry of beliefs, offering profound insights into reality, consciousness, and the human condition.

In Hinduism, the principle of karma stands as a cornerstone of synchronicity. It posits that every action, thought, and word leaves an indelible mark on the soul, shaping individual destinies across lifetimes. The intricate web of cause and effect dictates the unfolding of events, as the repercussions of one's actions resonate through time and space, interlinking with the broader cosmic order.

In Buddhism, the concept of dependent origination underscores the interconnectedness of all phenomena. It elucidates how every event, no matter how seemingly insignificant, is intricately linked to a vast network of causes and conditions. This interconnected web of causality transcends individual boundaries, intertwining the fates of all beings in a ceaseless dance of existence.

Taoism offers yet another perspective on synchronicity, rooted in the notion of the Tao, the underlying principle of the universe. The Tao Te Ching, a foundational text of Taoist philosophy, speaks of the harmonious interplay of yin and yang, the complementary forces that underpin existence. Synchronicity, in this context, arises from the effortless alignment with the natural flow of the Tao, where actions unfold spontaneously in accordance with the rhythm of the cosmos.

In Confucianism, the concept of li embodies the principle of cosmic order and propriety. It emphasizes the importance of cultivating virtuous conduct and harmonious relationships within society. Synchronicity, within the Confucian framework, emerges from the alignment of individual actions with the broader moral order, where ethical conduct reverberates through the interconnected fabric of human relationships.

Across these diverse philosophical traditions, synchronicity serves as a guiding principle, illuminating the underlying unity of all existence. It reminds us that every thought, action, and intention ripples through the fabric of reality, shaping the course of our lives and the world around us. In embracing synchronicity, we acknowledge our interconnectedness with the cosmos, surrendering to the mysterious dance of life's unfolding.

Synchronicity transcends cultural and religious boundaries, offering a universal framework for understanding the interconnected nature of reality. Whether through the lens of Hindu karma, Buddhist dependent origination, Taoist harmony, or Confucian propriety, synchronicity speaks to the fundamental interdependence of all phenomena.

In the modern world, the concept of synchronicity continues to resonate, finding expression in fields ranging from psychology to quantum physics. Carl Jung, the renowned Swiss psychologist, introduced the term synchronicity to Western audiences, highlighting the meaningful coincidences that defy conventional notions of causality. For Jung, synchronicity represented a bridge between the inner psyche and the outer world, a window into the deeper currents of the unconscious mind.

From a psychological perspective, synchronicity offers valuable insights into the interconnected nature of human experience. It invites us to explore the hidden patterns and connections that shape our lives, recognizing the significance of seemingly random events in the tapestry of our personal narratives. By attuning to synchronicity, we open ourselves to a deeper understanding of ourselves and the world around us, embracing the mystery and wonder of existence.

In the realm of quantum physics, the concept of synchronicity finds resonance in the notion of entanglement, where particles remain interconnected regardless of the distance between them. This phenomenon challenges our conventional understanding of space and time, suggesting a deeper unity underlying the fabric of reality. Synchronicity, in this context, hints at a profound interconnectedness that transcends the boundaries of classical physics, pointing towards a holistic understanding of the universe.

The concept of synchronicity offers a profound lens through which to explore the interconnected nature of reality. Across diverse philosophical traditions and modern scientific disciplines, synchronicity speaks to the underlying unity of all existence, inviting us to embrace the mysterious dance of life's unfolding. Whether through the principles of karma, dependent origination, harmony, or cosmic order, synchronicity reminds us of our interconnectedness with the cosmos, weaving a tapestry of meaning and significance that spans the depths of human experience.

The concept of synchronicity extends beyond individual experiences to encompass collective phenomena. In the realm of sociology and anthropology, synchronistic events often manifest as cultural myths, symbols, and rituals that bind communities together. These shared narratives and symbolic expressions reflect the interconnectedness of human consciousness, shaping collective identities and worldviews.

Anthropologist Joseph Campbell explored the role of synchronicity in mythology, highlighting the universal themes and archetypal motifs that recur across cultures and civilizations. Through his concept of the "hero's journey," Campbell identified a common thread of synchronistic encounters and transformative experiences that propel individuals towards self-discovery and spiritual awakening. These synchronistic moments serve as catalysts for personal growth and evolution, guiding individuals along their unique paths of self-realization.

In literature and the arts, synchronicity often manifests as creative inspiration and artistic expression. Writers, poets, and artists draw upon synchronistic experiences to infuse their work with depth, meaning, and resonance. The poet Rumi, for instance, spoke of the soul's journey towards union with the divine as a series of synchronistic encounters and mystical revelations. His poetry captures the essence of synchronicity, inviting readers to explore the interconnectedness of love, spirituality, and the human experience.

In music, synchronicity is evident in the harmonious interplay of melodies, rhythms, and harmonies that resonate with listeners on a profound emotional level. Jazz musicians, in particular, embrace the concept of synchronicity through improvisation, where individual players spontaneously respond to one another in the moment, creating a collective synergy that transcends individual skill. The music of John Coltrane, Miles Davis, and other jazz pioneers exemplifies the power of synchronicity to evoke transcendent states of consciousness and communal connection.

Furthermore, in the realm of ecology and environmentalism, synchronicity offers a framework for understanding the interconnectedness of ecosystems and the web of life. Ecologist Fritjof Capra introduced the concept of "deep ecology," which emphasizes the inherent value of all living beings and the interdependence of ecological systems. Synchronicity, in this context, reveals the intricate relationships between humans, nature, and the cosmos, underscoring the need for ecological stewardship and sustainability.

In the digital age, technology has facilitated new forms of synchronicity through social media, online communities, and virtual networks. The internet serves as a vast interconnected web of information and communication, where individuals from diverse backgrounds and cultures can connect and collaborate in real-time. Synchronistic encounters abound in the digital realm, as people serendipitously encounter ideas, opportunities, and connections that shape their lives in unexpected ways.

Recent advances in artificial intelligence and machine learning have led to the emergence of algorithmic synchronicity, where intelligent algorithms identify patterns and correlations in vast datasets, revealing hidden insights and opportunities. These algorithms power recommendation systems, personalized advertising, and predictive analytics, shaping our digital experiences and influencing our decision-making processes in subtle yet significant ways.

The concept of synchronicity continues to evolve and expand in the modern world, encompassing a wide range of disciplines and domains. From psychology and quantum physics to mythology and ecology, synchronicity offers a profound lens through which to explore the interconnected nature of reality. Whether through personal experiences, cultural expressions, or technological innovations, synchronicity reminds us of the underlying unity of all existence, inviting us to embrace the mystery and wonder of life's unfolding journey.

The concept of synchronicity intersects with contemporary approaches to wellness and holistic healing. In alternative medicine and integrative health practices, synchronicity is often invoked to explain the interconnectedness of mind, body, and spirit in the healing process. Modalities such as acupuncture, yoga, and meditation emphasize the importance of aligning with the natural rhythms of the body and the universe, fostering a state of balance and harmony conducive to healing and well-being.

In the field of psychotherapy, synchronicity plays a significant role in the therapeutic process, providing insights and breakthroughs that transcend rational explanation.

Jungian analysts, in particular, incorporate synchronicity into their therapeutic approach, recognizing the symbolic significance of coincidences and meaningful patterns in clients' lives. By exploring these synchronistic experiences, therapists can help clients gain deeper insights into their unconscious motivations, unresolved conflicts, and spiritual aspirations.

Furthermore, in the realm of education and learning, synchronicity offers a framework for understanding the interconnected nature of knowledge and wisdom. Educators who embrace a holistic approach to teaching and learning recognize the importance of fostering synchronistic encounters and transformative experiences in the classroom. By creating environments that encourage curiosity, exploration, and serendipitous discovery, educators can inspire students to make meaningful connections between diverse fields of study and to cultivate a lifelong love of learning.

In the domain of business and entrepreneurship, synchronicity often manifests as serendipitous opportunities, chance encounters, and unexpected breakthroughs that propel individuals and organizations towards success. Visionary leaders recognize the importance of remaining open to synchronistic events and intuitive insights in navigating complex challenges and seizing emerging opportunities. By cultivating a culture of innovation, collaboration, and adaptability, businesses can harness the power of synchronicity to drive creative solutions and sustainable growth.

In the realm of politics and social activism, synchronicity can serve as a catalyst for collective transformation and social change. Movements for justice, equality, and sustainability often emerge from synchronistic encounters, shared visions, and collective aspirations for a better world. By fostering connections, solidarity, and mutual support among diverse stakeholders, activists can harness the power of synchronicity to effect positive change on local, national, and global scales.

The concept of synchronicity offers a multifaceted lens through which to explore the interconnected nature of reality across diverse domains and disciplines. Whether in the realms of health and wellness, psychology and therapy, education and learning, business and entrepreneurship, or politics and social activism, synchronicity invites us to embrace the mystery and wonder of life's unfolding journey. By recognizing the meaningful connections and serendipitous encounters that shape our lives, we can cultivate a deeper sense of purpose, meaning, and interconnectedness in our individual and collective endeavors.

Additionally, in the realm of spirituality and personal growth, synchronicity serves as a guiding principle for those on a journey of self-discovery and inner transformation. Spiritual seekers and practitioners of various traditions often interpret synchronistic events as signs or messages from the universe, guiding them along their path towards enlightenment or spiritual awakening. These synchronistic encounters may take the form of meaningful coincidences, synchronistic dreams, or encounters with spiritual teachers and mentors who offer guidance and support on the journey inward.

In the field of parapsychology and the study of psi phenomena, synchronicity offers intriguing insights into the nature of consciousness and the interconnectedness of mind and matter. Researchers investigate phenomena such as telepathy, precognition, and psychokinesis, seeking to understand the underlying mechanisms that govern these seemingly anomalous experiences. Synchronicity, in this context, suggests a deeper interplay between the individual psyche and the broader field of consciousness, challenging conventional notions of causality and determinism.

Furthermore, in the realm of cultural studies and media analysis, synchronicity provides a framework for understanding the pervasive influence of symbols, archetypes, and narratives in shaping collective beliefs and behaviors. Cultural theorists explore the role of synchronicity in the production and consumption of media, examining how synchronistic encounters with books, films, and artworks can evoke profound emotional responses and transformative insights. By studying the ways in which synchronicity operates within cultural discourse, researchers gain valuable insights into the dynamics of power, representation, and social change.

In the field of astronomy and cosmology, synchronicity offers a lens through which to contemplate the mysteries of the universe and our place within it. Astrophysicists and cosmologists study the intricate patterns and structures of the cosmos, seeking to unravel the origins and evolution of the universe. Synchronicity, in this context, hints at a deeper cosmic order that transcends our limited understanding of space and time, inviting us to contemplate the interconnectedness of galaxies, stars, and planets on a grand cosmic scale.

In the realm of philosophy and metaphysics, synchronicity prompts profound questions about the nature of reality and the fabric of existence. Philosophers explore concepts such as the multiverse, parallel dimensions, and non-locality, seeking to reconcile the apparent randomness of quantum phenomena with the underlying order and coherence of the cosmos. Synchronicity, in this philosophical inquiry, serves as a bridge between the microcosm and the macrocosm, inviting us to contemplate the deeper mysteries of consciousness and creation.

The concept of synchronicity encompasses a vast spectrum of phenomena and disciplines, offering a rich tapestry of insights into the interconnected nature of reality. Whether explored through spirituality and personal growth, parapsychology and psi phenomena, cultural studies and media analysis, astronomy and cosmology, or philosophy and metaphysics, synchronicity invites us to explore the mysteries of existence with curiosity, wonder, and open-mindedness. By embracing synchronicity in all its forms, we can deepen our understanding of ourselves, our world, and the profound interconnectedness that binds us all together in the cosmic dance of life.

Chapter 14 - The Enigma of Time: Temporality and Synchronistic Events

Time, that elusive river flowing inexorably forward, has long fascinated and perplexed humanity. From the ancient philosophers pondering the nature of eternity to modern physicists probing the fabric of space-time, the enigma of time continues to captivate our imaginations. Within this intricate tapestry of temporal intricacies, the phenomenon of synchronicity emerges as a mysterious thread, weaving through the fabric of reality and challenging our understanding of causality and destiny.

At its core, synchronicity involves meaningful coincidences that seem to defy conventional explanations, occurring across the vast expanse of time and space. Unlike mere chance occurrences, synchronistic events carry a sense of significance or resonance, often manifesting as uncanny parallels or serendipitous encounters. The question of how time intersects with synchronicity raises profound metaphysical and philosophical implications, inviting us to explore the mysteries of temporal dynamics and the nature of reality itself.

One of the key aspects of synchronistic events is their seemingly non-linear relationship with time. While traditional cause-and-effect relationships operate within the framework of linear time, synchronicity suggests a deeper, more intricate relationship between inner and outer events. Carl Jung, the Swiss psychiatrist who coined the term synchronicity, proposed that these meaningful coincidences arise from the interconnectedness of the collective unconscious, where archetypal patterns and universal symbols intersect with individual lives. In this view, time becomes a fluid and multidimensional tapestry, where past, present, and future intertwine in a dance of cosmic significance.

The notion of synchronicity challenges our linear conception of time, suggesting that events may be connected across different points in time in ways that transcend our ordinary understanding. For example, a dream that foreshadows a future event or a chance encounter that echoes a past experience hints at the non-linear nature of time and the mysterious ways in which causality operates beyond our grasp. By embracing the enigma of time, we open ourselves to the possibility of a reality that transcends the confines of linear progression, where past, present, and future coalesce in a timeless dance of synchronicity.

From a quantum perspective, the relationship between time and synchronicity becomes even more intriguing. Quantum theory challenges our classical notions of time as a linear progression, suggesting that the past, present, and future may coexist simultaneously in a state of quantum superposition. According to this view, events may be connected across time through quantum entanglement, where particles become correlated in such a way that their states are intimately linked regardless of the distance between them. This quantum entanglement may provide a potential mechanism for synchronicity, whereby meaningful coincidences arise from the entangled nature of reality.

Besides its metaphysical implications, the enigma of time and synchronicity raises profound questions about the nature of reality and human consciousness. Are we mere spectators passively observing the unfolding drama of existence, or do we play an active role in shaping our destinies through the power of intention and awareness? By exploring the mysteries of time and synchronicity, we gain insights into the interconnectedness of all things and our place within the cosmic tapestry of existence.

The enigma of time and synchronicity invites us to reconsider our understanding of reality and the nature of causality. As we peer into the depths of temporal intricacies, we are confronted with the mystery of synchronicity, where meaningful coincidences bridge the gap between past, present, and future. By embracing the enigma of time, we open ourselves to the transformative power of synchronicity, unlocking new possibilities for self-discovery, growth, and spiritual awakening.

The concept of time has been a perennial source of fascination and bewilderment for humanity throughout the ages. From the musings of ancient philosophers contemplating eternity to the cutting-edge investigations of modern physicists probing the fabric of space-time, the mystery of time continues to captivate our minds. Within this vast landscape of temporal complexity, the phenomenon of synchronicity emerges as a mysterious thread, intricately woven into the fabric of reality, challenging our conventional notions of causality and destiny.

At its heart, synchronicity encompasses meaningful coincidences that defy simple explanations, occurring across the vast expanse of time and space. Unlike random chance occurrences, synchronistic events carry a sense of significance or resonance, often appearing as uncanny parallels or serendipitous encounters. The intersection of time with synchronicity raises profound metaphysical and philosophical questions, prompting us to delve into the mysteries of temporal dynamics and the very nature of reality itself.

A central aspect of synchronistic events lies in their seemingly non-linear relationship with time. While traditional cause-and-effect relationships adhere to the linear progression of time, synchronicity suggests a deeper, more intricate connection between inner and outer events. Carl Jung, the Swiss psychiatrist who introduced the concept of synchronicity, proposed that these meaningful coincidences arise from the interconnectedness of the collective unconscious, where archetypal patterns and universal symbols intersect with individual lives. In this view, time takes on a fluid and multidimensional quality, with past, present, and future intermingling in a cosmic dance of significance.

The notion of synchronicity challenges our linear conception of time, suggesting that events may be linked across different temporal points in ways that transcend our ordinary understanding. For instance, a dream foretelling a future event or a chance encounter echoing a past experience hints at the non-linear nature of time and the mysterious workings of causality beyond our grasp. By embracing the enigma of time, we open ourselves to the possibility of a reality that transcends the confines of linear progression, where past, present, and future merge in a timeless symphony of synchronicity.

From a quantum perspective, the relationship between time and synchronicity takes on an even more intriguing dimension. Quantum theory disrupts our classical notions of time as a linear flow, proposing instead that the past, present, and future may exist simultaneously in a state of quantum superposition. According to this framework, events can be connected across time through quantum entanglement, where particles become correlated in such a way that their states are intimately linked regardless of spatial separation. This quantum entanglement offers a potential mechanism for synchronicity, whereby meaningful coincidences arise from the entangled nature of reality itself.

The enigma of time and synchronicity beckons us to reexamine our understanding of reality and the mechanics of causality. As we peer into the depths of temporal complexities, we encounter the mystery of synchronicity, where meaningful coincidences serve as bridges between past, present, and future. Embracing the enigma of time opens doors to the transformative power of synchronicity, unlocking new avenues for self-discovery, growth, and spiritual enlightenment.

Furthermore, the interplay between time and synchronicity extends beyond theoretical speculation to practical applications in various fields of study and human experience. In psychology, for instance, the exploration of synchronicity offers valuable insights into the workings of the human mind and the interconnectedness of conscious and unconscious processes. Therapists and counselors often integrate the concept of synchronicity into their practice, helping clients recognize and explore meaningful coincidences as pathways to self-discovery and healing.

In the realm of literature and the arts, synchronicity serves as a rich source of inspiration and creative expression. Writers, poets, and artists draw upon synchronistic experiences to infuse their work with depth, meaning, and resonance. From the surreal imagery of Salvador Dalí to the mystical poetry of William Blake, synchronicity manifests in myriad forms, inviting audiences to ponder the mysteries of existence and the interconnectedness of all things.

In the realm of education and learning, synchronicity offers a framework for understanding the interconnected nature of knowledge and wisdom. Educators who embrace a holistic approach to teaching recognize the importance of fostering synchronistic encounters and transformative experiences in the classroom. By creating environments that encourage curiosity, exploration, and serendipitous discovery, educators can inspire students to make meaningful connections between diverse fields of study and to cultivate a lifelong love of learning.

In the realm of technology and innovation, synchronicity plays a subtle yet significant role in shaping the development of new ideas and discoveries. Innovators and inventors often speak of moments of synchronicity that lead to breakthroughs and insights that defy conventional explanation. These serendipitous encounters may occur during moments of collaboration, experimentation, or even chance encounters, highlighting the interconnected nature of creativity and discovery.

Furthermore, in the field of parapsychology and the study of psi phenomena, synchronicity offers intriguing insights into the nature of consciousness and the interconnectedness of mind and matter. Researchers investigate phenomena such as telepathy, precognition, and psychokinesis, seeking to understand the underlying mechanisms that govern these seemingly anomalous experiences. Synchronicity, in this context, suggests a deeper interplay between the individual psyche and the broader field of consciousness, challenging conventional notions of causality and determinism.

The concept of synchronicity transcends disciplinary boundaries, offering a multifaceted lens through which to explore the interconnected nature of reality. Whether in psychology, literature, education, technology, spirituality, or parapsychology, synchronicity invites us to embrace the mystery and wonder of existence with curiosity, wonder, and open-mindedness. By recognizing the meaningful connections and serendipitous encounters that shape our lives, we can cultivate a deeper sense of purpose, meaning, and interconnectedness in our individual and collective endeavors.

The phenomenon of synchronicity has profound implications for our understanding of relationships and social dynamics. In sociology and anthropology, synchronistic events often manifest as cultural myths, symbols, and rituals that bind communities together. These shared narratives and symbolic expressions reflect the interconnectedness of human consciousness, shaping collective identities and worldviews. By studying the role of synchronicity in cultural practices and social institutions, researchers gain insights into the ways in which meaningful coincidences contribute to the cohesion and resilience of societies.

In the realm of ecology and environmentalism, synchronicity offers a lens through which to contemplate the interconnectedness of ecosystems and the web of life. Ecologists and conservationists recognize the importance of synchronistic relationships in maintaining the balance and vitality of natural systems. By studying the intricate patterns and dynamics of ecological synchrony, researchers gain insights into the ways in which species coexist and interact within their respective habitats. The recognition of synchronicity in nature inspires a deeper reverence and stewardship for the Earth and all its inhabitants, fostering a sense of interconnectedness and responsibility towards the planet.

Furthermore, in the realm of politics and social activism, synchronicity can serve as a catalyst for collective transformation and social change. Movements for justice, equality, and sustainability often emerge from synchronistic encounters, shared visions, and collective aspirations for a better world. By fostering connections, solidarity, and mutual support among diverse stakeholders, activists can harness the power of synchronicity to effect positive change on local, national, and global scales. The recognition of synchronicity in social movements underscores the interconnectedness of individual actions and collective outcomes, highlighting the importance of collaboration and solidarity in creating a more just and sustainable society.

In the realm of business and entrepreneurship, synchronicity often manifests as serendipitous opportunities, chance encounters, and unexpected breakthroughs that propel individuals and organizations towards success. Visionary leaders recognize the importance of remaining open to synchronistic events and intuitive insights in navigating complex challenges and seizing emerging opportunities. By cultivating a culture of innovation, collaboration, and adaptability, businesses can harness the power of synchronicity to drive creative solutions and sustainable growth. The recognition of synchronicity in business fosters an entrepreneurial mindset that embraces uncertainty and embraces the potential for transformative change.

In the realm of healthcare and wellness, synchronicity offers a framework for understanding the interconnected nature of mind, body, and spirit in the healing process. Integrative medicine practitioners recognize the importance of addressing the root causes of illness and disease, which may extend beyond the physical body to include emotional, mental, and spiritual factors. By incorporating holistic approaches that honor the interconnectedness of all aspects of being, healthcare providers can support patients in achieving optimal health and well-being. The recognition of synchronicity in healing practices fosters a deeper sense of connection and empowerment for both patients and practitioners, leading to more effective and transformative outcomes.

In summary, the concept of synchronicity offers a profound lens through which to explore the interconnected nature of reality across diverse domains and disciplines. Whether in sociology and anthropology, ecology and environmentalism, politics and social activism, business and entrepreneurship, or healthcare and wellness, synchronicity invites us to recognize the meaningful connections and serendipitous encounters that shape our lives. By embracing synchronicity in all its forms, we can cultivate a deeper sense of purpose, meaning, and interconnectedness in our individual and collective endeavors, leading to more harmonious and sustainable ways of living on this planet.

Chapter 15 - The Butterfly Effect: Chaos Theory and Synchronicity

In the intricate web of existence, seemingly insignificant events can have far-reaching consequences, setting off a chain reaction of cause and effect that reverberates across time and space. This phenomenon, known as the butterfly effect, lies at the heart of chaos theory, a branch of mathematics and physics that explores the behavior of complex systems. Within the context of synchronicity, the butterfly effect offers intriguing insights into the interconnectedness of all things and the mysterious ways in which seemingly unrelated events can converge to shape our destinies.

The concept of the butterfly effect originates from the field of meteorology, where it was first proposed by mathematician and meteorologist Edward Lorenz in the 1960s. Lorenz discovered that small changes in the initial conditions of a weather system could lead to drastically different outcomes, illustrating the sensitivity of complex systems to initial perturbations. He famously remarked that the flapping of a butterfly's wings in Brazil could set off a tornado in Texas, highlighting the nonlinear dynamics of chaotic systems.

In the context of synchronicity, the butterfly effect suggests that seemingly random events may be interconnected in subtle and meaningful ways, giving rise to synchronistic phenomena that transcend conventional notions of cause and effect. For example, a chance encounter with a stranger may lead to a life-changing opportunity, or a seemingly insignificant decision may alter the course of one's destiny. These synchronistic events echo the butterfly effect, where small perturbations in the fabric of reality can lead to profound and unexpected outcomes.

The butterfly effect also underscores the interconnectedness of all things, illustrating how individual actions can ripple outward to influence the broader context of existence. Just as a butterfly's wings can set off a chain reaction of atmospheric disturbances, so too can our thoughts, emotions, and intentions create waves of influence that shape the world around us. In this view, synchronicity arises from the intricate interplay of myriad factors, converging to create moments of significance and resonance.

From a scientific perspective, chaos theory offers a framework for understanding the underlying dynamics of synchronistic events. Complex systems, such as the weather, the stock market, or the human brain, exhibit nonlinear behavior that can give rise to unexpected patterns and phenomena. By studying the underlying principles of chaos theory, scientists can gain insights into the emergence of synchronicity and its implications for our understanding of reality.

Besides its scientific implications, the butterfly effect and chaos theory also have profound philosophical and spiritual significance. They remind us of the interconnectedness of all things and the inherent unpredictability of existence. Synchronistic events, with their mysterious confluence of factors, invite us to embrace the uncertainty of life and to recognize the hidden patterns and connections that underlie our experiences.

The butterfly effect and chaos theory offer intriguing parallels to the phenomenon of synchronicity, shedding light on the interconnected nature of reality and the mysterious ways in which seemingly random events can converge to shape our lives. By exploring the dynamics of complex systems, we gain insights into the emergence of synchronicity and its profound implications for our understanding of causality, destiny, and the nature of existence.

The concept of the butterfly effect finds its roots in meteorology, where it was initially postulated by mathematician and meteorologist Edward Lorenz during the 1960s. Lorenz's groundbreaking insights revealed that minute alterations in the initial conditions of a weather system could yield vastly divergent outcomes, demonstrating the sensitivity of complex systems to minuscule perturbations. His famous analogy likening the fluttering of a butterfly's wings in Brazil to the formation of a tornado in Texas underscores the nonlinear dynamics inherent in chaotic systems.

In the context of synchronicity, the butterfly effect intimates that ostensibly random occurrences may possess subtle yet profound connections, giving rise to synchronistic phenomena that transcend conventional causality. For instance, a chance encounter with a stranger might catalyze a life-altering opportunity, or a seemingly trivial decision could redirect the trajectory of one's destiny. These synchronistic episodes mirror the butterfly effect, wherein minor disturbances in the fabric of reality can engender momentous and unforeseen outcomes.

The butterfly effect underscores the interconnected nature of all phenomena, illustrating how individual actions can cascade outward to influence the broader tapestry of existence. Just as the fluttering of a butterfly's wings can trigger a sequence of atmospheric disturbances, so too can our thoughts, emotions, and intentions propagate waves of influence that shape the world around us. From this perspective, synchronicity emerges from the intricate interplay of myriad variables, converging to manifest moments of significance and resonance.

From a scientific standpoint, chaos theory furnishes a framework for comprehending the underlying mechanisms of synchronistic events. Complex systems, such as weather patterns, financial markets, or neural networks, exhibit nonlinear behavior that can engender unexpected patterns and occurrences. Through the exploration of the fundamental tenets of chaos theory, scientists can glean insights into the genesis of synchronicity and its ramifications for our comprehension of reality.

Beyond its scientific implications, the butterfly effect and chaos theory harbor profound philosophical and spiritual connotations. They serve as poignant reminders of the interconnectedness of all phenomena and the intrinsic unpredictability of existence. Synchronistic occurrences, with their mysterious confluence of elements, beckon us to embrace the uncertainties of life and to discern the concealed patterns and connections that underpin our experiences.

The butterfly effect and chaos theory offer striking parallels to the phenomenon of synchronicity, shedding light on the interwoven fabric of reality and the cryptic ways in which ostensibly fortuitous events coalesce to mold our destinies. Through the exploration of complex systems, we gain insights into the genesis of synchronicity and its profound implications for our comprehension of causality, destiny, and the essence of being.

Furthermore, delving deeper into the implications of the butterfly effect and chaos theory unveils intriguing insights into various aspects of human existence, spanning realms beyond the scientific. In the domain of psychology, for instance, these concepts offer a lens through which to examine the complexities of human behavior and cognition. Just as small perturbations in a system can lead to significant outcomes, subtle shifts in thoughts, emotions, and perceptions can ripple outward to influence our actions and experiences. Understanding the dynamics of chaos theory can thus provide psychologists with valuable tools for comprehending the intricacies of the human mind and the emergence of synchronistic phenomena within personal and interpersonal realms.

In the realm of creativity and innovation, the principles of chaos theory and the butterfly effect illuminate the process by which novel ideas and breakthroughs emerge. Creative endeavors often unfold in nonlinear, unpredictable ways, with inspiration striking seemingly out of nowhere. By embracing the inherent uncertainty and complexity of creative processes, individuals and teams can cultivate environments conducive to innovation and discovery. Recognizing the potential for synchronistic connections to emerge amidst chaos fosters a mindset of openness and receptivity, allowing for the emergence of transformative insights and solutions.

In the context of relationships and social dynamics, the butterfly effect and chaos theory offer valuable insights into the interconnected nature of human interactions. Just as small actions can have far-reaching consequences in complex systems, individual behaviors and choices can reverberate throughout social networks, shaping the collective experiences of communities and societies. By fostering an awareness of the ripple effects of our actions, individuals can cultivate empathy, compassion, and mindfulness in their interactions with others, nurturing harmonious and resilient social ecosystems.

Furthermore, in the realm of spirituality and personal growth, the principles embodied by the butterfly effect and chaos theory resonate deeply with teachings from various wisdom traditions. Concepts such as karma, interconnectedness, and the law of attraction mirror the interconnected dynamics elucidated by chaos theory, highlighting the profound implications of our thoughts, intentions, and actions. By embracing the idea that we are co-creators of our reality, individuals can cultivate a sense of empowerment and responsibility for shaping their destinies in alignment with higher principles of harmony and wholeness.

Besides, the principles of chaos theory and the butterfly effect hold relevance for broader societal issues, such as environmental sustainability and global interconnectedness. Recognizing the interconnected nature of ecological systems and human societies underscores the importance of adopting holistic, systems-based approaches to addressing complex challenges such as climate change, biodiversity loss, and social inequality. By acknowledging the butterfly effect inherent in our collective actions and decisions, we can cultivate a deeper sense of stewardship for the planet and a commitment to fostering resilience and thriving for all life forms.

The butterfly effect and chaos theory offer profound insights into the interconnected nature of reality and the mysterious ways in which seemingly insignificant events can cascade to shape our lives and the world around us. By exploring the implications of these concepts across diverse domains, from psychology and creativity to relationships and spirituality, we gain a deeper appreciation for the intricacies of existence and our role as active participants in the unfolding tapestry of life. Embracing the inherent uncertainty and complexity of chaos, we can cultivate a mindset of openness, curiosity, and adaptability, fostering a deeper sense of connection, creativity, and resilience in our personal and collective journeys.

Furthermore, the principles of chaos theory and the butterfly effect have profound implications for the field of education and learning. By understanding the nonlinear dynamics of knowledge acquisition and cognitive development, educators can design learning experiences that harness the power of uncertainty and complexity. Rather than adhering to rigid, linear models of instruction, educators can embrace dynamic, interactive approaches that allow for emergent learning and creative problem solving. In doing so, students are encouraged to explore, experiment, and make connections across disciplines, fostering a deeper understanding of the interconnected nature of knowledge and the world around them.

In the realm of economics and business, the principles of chaos theory offer valuable insights into the dynamics of markets and organizational behavior. Economic systems are inherently complex, characterized by nonlinear interactions between various factors such as supply and demand, investor sentiment, and government policies. By recognizing the emergent patterns and behaviors that arise from these interactions, economists and business leaders can develop more resilient and adaptive strategies for navigating uncertain and turbulent environments. Embracing the inherent unpredictability of economic systems opens doors to innovative approaches to risk management, decision-making, and organizational design.

In the realm of health and wellness, chaos theory provides a framework for understanding the dynamics of complex biological systems, such as the human body and ecosystems. From the fractal patterns of the cardiovascular system to the self-organizing properties of the immune system, biological systems exhibit nonlinear behavior that can be influenced by a myriad of factors, including genetics, environment, and lifestyle. By studying the underlying principles of chaos theory, healthcare practitioners can gain insights into the interconnected dynamics of health and disease, informing more holistic and personalized approaches to diagnosis, treatment, and prevention.

Furthermore, in the realm of technology and innovation, chaos theory and the butterfly effect inspire novel approaches to problem solving and design. Just as small changes in initial conditions can lead to significant outcomes in complex systems, minor adjustments in algorithms, user interfaces, or design elements can profoundly affect the user experience and the success of a product or service. By embracing the inherent uncertainty and complexity of technological systems, engineers and designers can cultivate a mindset of experimentation and adaptation, leading to more resilient and user-centric innovations.

Additionally, the principles of chaos theory and the butterfly effect have implications for the study of consciousness and the nature of reality. From the fractal patterns of neural networks to the self-organizing properties of consciousness itself, the dynamics of consciousness exhibit nonlinear behavior that defies conventional explanation. By exploring the parallels between chaos theory and the dynamics of consciousness, researchers can gain insights into the interconnected nature of mind and matter, opening new avenues for understanding the mysteries of human consciousness and the fabric of existence.

The butterfly effect and chaos theory offer profound insights into the interconnected nature of reality and the mysterious ways in which seemingly insignificant events can cascade to shape our lives and the world around us. By exploring the implications of these concepts across diverse domains, from education and economics to health and technology, we gain a deeper appreciation for the intricate interplay of uncertainty and complexity in all aspects of existence. Embracing the inherent unpredictability of chaos, we can cultivate a mindset of openness, creativity, and resilience, empowering us to navigate the complexities of life with courage and curiosity.

Chapter 16 - Probability vs. Possibility: Reimagining Reality through Synchronicity

In the realm of synchronicity, the distinction between probability and possibility becomes blurred, inviting us to reimagine reality beyond the constraints of conventional logic and rationality. While probability deals with the likelihood of events occurring within a given framework of causality, possibility encompasses the realm of infinite potential and the mysterious interplay of chance and destiny. Within this fertile landscape of possibility, synchronicity emerges as a potent force, shaping our experiences and perceptions in ways that transcend the boundaries of ordinary reality.

Probability, rooted in the principles of statistics and mathematical analysis, offers a framework for understanding the likelihood of events occurring based on empirical data and observed patterns. From coin tosses to card games, probability provides a tool for quantifying the likelihood of various outcomes and making informed decisions in uncertain situations. While probability offers a valuable tool for predicting and understanding the likelihood of events in a deterministic universe, it falls short in capturing the full complexity and richness of synchronicity. Unlike probability, which operates within the confines of linear causality and predictable outcomes, synchronicity transcends traditional notions of cause and effect, encompassing the mysterious interplay of meaning, significance, and interconnectedness that underlies the fabric of reality. In this sense, synchronicity invites us to reimagine reality not as a fixed and deterministic system governed by probabilistic laws, but as a dynamic and interconnected web of possibilities where the boundaries between past, present, and future blur, and the unimaginable becomes possible. By embracing the enigmatic nature of synchronicity and its potential to transform our understanding of reality, we embark on a journey of exploration and discovery, venturing into the uncharted territories of consciousness, creativity, and the human spirit.

In the ethereal domain of synchronicity, the lines between probability and possibility dissolve, urging us to reconceptualize existence beyond the confines of conventional reasoning and logic. While probability delves into the likelihood of events unfolding within a structured framework of cause and effect, possibility stretches across the vast expanse of potentiality, where chance and fate intertwine in mysterious ways. Amidst this boundless realm of possibility, synchronicity emerges as a formidable force, molding our perceptions and encounters in ways that defy the limitations of ordinary reality.

Probability, grounded in statistical principles and mathematical analyses, provides a means of comprehending the chances of events materializing based on observed data and patterns. From the toss of a coin to the shuffle of cards in a game, probability furnishes us with a tool to assess the likelihood of diverse outcomes and to navigate through uncertainty with discernment. Nevertheless, while probability furnishes a valuable instrument for forecasting and comprehending the probabilities of occurrences within a deterministic cosmos, it falters in capturing the intricate depth and complexity of synchronicity. Unlike probability, which operates within the confines of a linear causal chain and foreseeable consequences, synchronicity transcends conventional cause-and-effect paradigms, embracing the enigmatic interplay of significance, meaning, and interconnectedness that underpins the very fabric of reality. In essence, synchronicity beckons us to envision reality not as a rigid and predetermined construct governed by probabilistic laws, but as a fluid and interconnected tapestry of potentialities where the boundaries between past, present, and future blur, and the inconceivable unfolds. By embracing the enigmatic essence of synchronicity and its capacity to revolutionize our perception of reality, we embark on a voyage of exploration and revelation, venturing into uncharted territories of consciousness, ingenuity, and the human essence.

In the grand tapestry of existence, synchronicity operates as a silent orchestrator, weaving together the threads of our lives in intricate patterns that defy rational explanation. It manifests as those moments of serendipity when events align in uncanny ways, leaving us awestruck by the seemingly choreographed dance of the universe. These synchronistic occurrences often carry a profound sense of significance or resonance, serving as signposts on our journey of self-discovery and growth.

While probability offers a framework for understanding the statistical likelihood of events within a causal framework, synchronicity transcends such linear models, hinting at a deeper underlying order beyond our comprehension. It suggests that there is a hidden harmony guiding the unfolding of events, a cosmic symphony in which each individual plays a unique part. This notion challenges our conventional notions of reality, inviting us to entertain the possibility of a universe imbued with meaning and purpose.

Carl Jung, the renowned Swiss psychiatrist and psychoanalyst, introduced the concept of synchronicity to the modern world, recognizing it as a phenomenon that defied conventional scientific explanation. He described synchronicity as meaningful coincidences that occur with no discernible causal connection, pointing to the existence of a collective unconscious that transcends individual experience. Jung believed that these synchronistic experiences could offer insights into the deeper patterns and archetypes that shape human existence, serving as windows into the mysteries of the psyche.

In the realm of quantum physics, synchronicity finds resonance in the concept of entanglement, where particles separated by vast distances can instantaneously influence each other's states. This phenomenon challenges our understanding of space and time, suggesting that there may be hidden connections linking all phenomena in the universe. While quantum mechanics operates on a scale far removed from our everyday experience, its implications for the nature of reality are profound, hinting at a universe far stranger and more interconnected than we can imagine.

Skeptics may dismiss synchronicity as mere coincidence or wishful thinking, attributing meaning to random events in an attempt to impose order on chaos. For those who have experienced synchronicity firsthand, it is often accompanied by a deep sense of resonance and intuition that transcends rational explanation. Whether it's a chance encounter that leads to a life-changing opportunity or a series of events that seem to unfold with uncanny precision, synchronicity has a way of reminding us that there is more to reality than meets the eye.

In the midst of life's uncertainties and challenges, synchronicity offers a glimmer of hope and possibility, reminding us that we are part of something greater than ourselves. It invites us to embrace the mystery and wonder of existence, opening ourselves to the magic that lies beyond the veil of the ordinary. By cultivating a sense of openness and receptivity to synchronistic experiences, we may discover a deeper sense of purpose and connection in our lives, guided by the invisible hand of fate.

Whether we choose to interpret synchronicity as a meaningful aspect of reality or dismiss it as mere coincidence is a matter of personal perspective. Yet, as we navigate the complexities of existence, it is worth considering the profound implications of synchronicity for our understanding of ourselves and the world around us. For in the dance of synchronicity, we may glimpse the hidden order that unites us all, offering a glimpse of the interconnected web of life in which we are but fleeting participants.

Exploring the phenomenon of synchronicity requires a willingness to embrace uncertainty and to relinquish the rigid boundaries of conventional thought. It challenges us to expand our consciousness and to perceive reality through a different lens, one that acknowledges the interconnectedness of all things. In doing so, we may come to recognize that synchronicity is not a rare occurrence reserved for the chosen few but rather an inherent aspect of the human experience, waiting to be acknowledged and explored.

One of the keys to unlocking the mysteries of synchronicity lies in cultivating a state of mindfulness and awareness in our daily lives. By paying attention to the subtle signs and symbols that surround us, we may begin to discern the underlying patterns and meanings that emerge. This heightened sense of awareness allows us to tune into the synchronistic currents that flow through our lives, guiding us on our journey with a sense of purpose and direction.

Art, literature, and mythology are rich sources of synchronistic symbolism, offering glimpses into the deeper truths that lie beyond the surface of reality. Archetypal motifs such as the hero's journey, the wise old sage, and the dark night of the soul resonate across cultures and epochs, reflecting universal themes of transformation and redemption. By delving into these timeless narratives, we may gain insights into our own life's journey and the challenges that we face along the way.

Creativity, too, is intimately connected with the phenomenon of synchronicity, serving as a channel through which the unseen forces of the universe may express themselves. Many artists, writers, and musicians speak of moments of inspiration that seem to come from beyond themselves, as if they are tapping into a deeper wellspring of creativity that transcends individual consciousness. In such moments, the boundaries between the self and the other dissolve, giving rise to works of art that resonate with a sense of universal truth and beauty.

Relationships can also be fertile ground for synchronistic encounters, as we are drawn into the lives of others in ways that defy rational explanation. Whether it's meeting a kindred spirit who shares our passions and interests or experiencing a chance encounter with a stranger who imparts wisdom that resonates deeply, synchronicity has a way of bringing people together in meaningful ways. These connections remind us that we are not alone in our journey and that we are all interconnected in ways that we may not fully understand.

In the search for meaning and purpose in our lives, synchronicity offers a beacon of light amidst the darkness, guiding us towards a deeper understanding of ourselves and the world around us. It invites us to trust in the inherent wisdom of the universe and to surrender to the flow of life with open hearts and minds. By embracing synchronicity as a guiding principle in our lives, we may find ourselves on a path of self-discovery and transformation, leading us towards greater fulfillment and wholeness.

Synchronicity is a phenomenon that defies easy explanation, yet its presence can be felt in the subtle whispers of intuition, the serendipitous encounters that shape our lives, and the timeless truths that resonate across cultures and epochs. By opening ourselves to the possibility of synchronicity, we may come to see the world with fresh eyes and to embrace the mystery and wonder that lie at the heart of existence. For in the dance of synchronicity, we may find ourselves swept away on a journey of discovery and revelation, guided by the invisible hand of fate towards a deeper understanding of ourselves and our place in the universe.

Furthermore, the study of synchronicity intersects with various disciplines, including psychology, philosophy, and spirituality, each offering unique perspectives on this enigmatic phenomenon. From a psychological standpoint, synchronicity can be viewed as the manifestation of the unconscious mind, reflecting our deepest desires, fears, and aspirations in the external world. Jungian analysts often explore synchronistic experiences as a means of gaining insight into the psyche's hidden depths, uncovering patterns of meaning and symbolism that may lie beneath the surface of conscious awareness.

Philosophically, synchronicity raises profound questions about the nature of reality and the role of consciousness in shaping our perceptions of the world. Some philosophers argue that synchronicity points to a fundamental interconnectedness between mind and matter, suggesting that consciousness plays a central role in shaping the events that unfold around us. From this perspective, synchronicity is not merely a curious anomaly but rather a fundamental aspect of the fabric of reality, reflecting the underlying unity of all existence.

Spiritually, synchronicity is often interpreted as a sign of divine guidance or intervention, signaling a deeper alignment with the cosmic forces that govern the universe. Many spiritual traditions teach that the universe is infused with a higher intelligence or divine presence that orchestrates the events of our lives with purpose and intention. From this perspective, synchronicity is seen as a form of communication from the universe, offering guidance and support on our spiritual journey towards wholeness and enlightenment.

Regardless of the lens through which we view synchronicity, one thing remains clear: it challenges us to expand our understanding of reality and to embrace the mysteries that lie beyond the confines of rational thought. In a world that often feels chaotic and unpredictable, synchronicity offers a glimmer of hope and meaning, reminding us that we are not alone in our journey and that there is a deeper order at work beneath the surface of reality. By opening ourselves to the possibility of synchronicity, we may find ourselves on a path of profound transformation and self-discovery, guided by the invisible hand of destiny towards a greater sense of purpose and fulfillment.

The exploration of synchronicity has practical implications for how we navigate our lives and make decisions. By attuning ourselves to the subtle cues and signs that may indicate a synchronistic occurrence, we can learn to trust our intuition and follow the flow of life with greater confidence. Rather than relying solely on logical reasoning and analysis, we can cultivate a deeper sense of trust in the unseen forces that guide our path, allowing us to make choices that are aligned with our true purpose and highest good.

In the realm of healing and personal growth, synchronicity can play a transformative role in facilitating healing and self-discovery. Many individuals report experiencing synchronistic events during times of profound change or spiritual awakening, serving as catalysts for inner transformation and growth. Whether it's a chance encounter with a wise mentor who offers guidance and support or a serendipitous opportunity that leads to a new path or direction in life, synchronicity has a way of opening doors and expanding our awareness of what is possible.

Furthermore, the study of synchronicity invites us to reconsider our relationship with time and space, challenging the linear concept of past, present, and future. In a synchronistic universe, time is not merely a linear progression but rather a fluid and dynamic continuum in which past, present, and future coexist in a timeless dance of interconnectedness. This perspective suggests that every moment is pregnant with possibility, and that the seeds of our future are sown in the present moment through the choices we make and the intentions we set.

From a quantum perspective, synchronicity finds resonance in the concept of quantum entanglement, where particles can become linked in such a way that the state of one particle instantaneously influences the state of another, regardless of the distance between them. This phenomenon challenges our understanding of causality and suggests that there may be hidden connections linking all phenomena in the universe. Just as particles can become entangled, so too can events and experiences in our lives become interconnected in ways that defy rational explanation, giving rise to synchronistic encounters that seem to transcend the limitations of time and space.

The study of synchronicity invites us to embrace a more expansive view of reality, one that acknowledges the interconnectedness of all things and the mysterious ways in which the universe communicates with us. Whether we interpret synchronicity as a product of the unconscious mind, a reflection of divine guidance, or a fundamental aspect of the fabric of reality, its presence in our lives serves as a reminder that we are part of something greater than ourselves. By opening ourselves to the possibility of synchronicity and trusting in the unseen forces that guide our path, we may find ourselves embarking on a journey of profound discovery and self-realization, guided by the invisible hand of destiny towards a deeper understanding of ourselves and our place in the universe.

Chapter 17 - Synchronicity in Relationships: Connections Beyond Rationality

In the intricate dance of human relationships, there exists a phenomenon that transcends mere chance encounters and logical explanations: synchronicity. Synchronicity in relationships refers to those meaningful coincidences, serendipitous encounters, and inexplicable connections that seem to defy rationality yet carry profound significance in the lives of those involved.

At the heart of synchronicity in relationships lies the idea that certain connections go beyond the surface level of causality or shared interests. Instead, they delve into the realm of the soul, resonating with a deeper, more profound sense of alignment and connection. These synchronistic experiences often occur when individuals are in a state of openness, vulnerability, or receptivity, allowing them to recognize and embrace the subtle threads that bind them to others.

One common example of synchronicity in relationships is the phenomenon of soulmates or kindred spirits—individuals who feel an instant, inexplicable connection upon meeting, as if they have known each other for lifetimes. These soul connections often transcend conventional notions of compatibility or attraction, encompassing a sense of recognition and resonance that defies rational explanation. Whether romantic partners, close friends, or spiritual allies, soulmates embody the essence of synchronicity in relationships, reminding us of the profound connections that exist beyond the realm of logic or reason.

Synchronicity in relationships can also manifest in the form of shared experiences, parallel journeys, or serendipitous encounters that seem to unfold with uncanny timing or precision. For example, two individuals may find themselves navigating similar challenges or life transitions simultaneously, offering each other support, guidance, and understanding along the way. These synchronistic parallels highlight the interconnectedness of human experience and the ways in which our paths intersect and intertwine with those of others.

Synchronicity in relationships often serves as a catalyst for personal growth, healing, and transformation. When individuals are attuned to the subtle synchronistic cues present in their relationships, they may uncover hidden patterns, unresolved emotions, or unhealed wounds that are seeking to be addressed. By recognizing and honoring these synchronistic messages, individuals can deepen their understanding of themselves and others, fostering greater intimacy, authenticity, and mutual support within their relationships.

It's important to note that synchronicity in relationships is not always easy to navigate, especially when it challenges our existing beliefs, expectations, or attachments. In some cases, synchronistic connections may trigger feelings of vulnerability, uncertainty, or fear as individuals confront aspects of themselves that have been hidden or denied. These shadow aspects, though uncomfortable to acknowledge, contain valuable insights and opportunities for growth if approached with courage, compassion, and self-awareness.

Synchronicity in relationships invites us to embrace the mystery and magic of human connection, recognizing that there are forces at work beyond our comprehension or control. By cultivating an attitude of openness, curiosity, and trust, individuals can attune themselves to the synchronistic currents flowing through their lives, allowing them to forge deeper, more meaningful connections with others and with themselves.

Synchronicity in relationships represents a profound invitation to explore the interconnectedness of human experience and the deeper dimensions of connection that lie beyond the realm of rationality or logic. By honoring the synchronistic cues present in our relationships, we can uncover hidden truths, foster greater intimacy, and embark on a journey of mutual growth and transformation.

Furthermore, synchronicity often serves as a catalyst for personal growth and transformation within relationships. By attuning themselves to synchronistic cues, individuals may uncover hidden patterns or unresolved emotions that are seeking acknowledgment. By embracing these synchronistic messages, individuals can deepen their understanding of themselves and others, fostering greater intimacy and authenticity in their relationships.

Navigating synchronicity in relationships isn't always easy, especially when it challenges our beliefs or triggers feelings of vulnerability. In some instances, synchronistic connections may unearth uncomfortable truths or shadow aspects of ourselves that we've long ignored. Yet, these moments of discomfort present opportunities for growth and self-discovery if approached with courage and self-awareness.

Synchronicity invites us to embrace the mystery and magic of human connection, acknowledging that there are forces at play beyond our comprehension. By cultivating openness and trust, individuals can tune into the synchronistic currents of their lives, forging deeper connections with others and embarking on a journey of mutual growth and transformation.

The exploration of synchronicity in relationships extends beyond individual connections to encompass broader themes of collective resonance and universal interconnectedness. In essence, it suggests that our interactions with others are not isolated incidents but rather part of a larger, cosmic dance in which every encounter carries significance and meaning. This perspective encourages us to view our relationships not as separate entities but as interconnected strands woven into the fabric of existence.

Consider, for example, how synchronicity can manifest within communities or social networks, where seemingly unrelated events or encounters converge to reveal underlying patterns or themes. These synchronous occurrences often serve as catalysts for collective growth and evolution, sparking a ripple effect of transformation that extends far beyond individual relationships. By recognizing and honoring these synchronistic patterns, communities can deepen their sense of cohesion and solidarity, fostering greater harmony and understanding among their members.

Furthermore, the study of synchronicity in relationships has profound implications for fields such as psychology, anthropology, and spirituality. Psychologists, for instance, may explore how synchronistic experiences contribute to individuals' sense of meaning and purpose in life, while anthropologists may investigate how synchronicity shapes cultural beliefs and practices surrounding relationships and human connection. Spiritual traditions from around the world have long recognized the significance of synchronicity as a guiding force in the unfoldment of human consciousness, offering practices and teachings aimed at attuning individuals to the subtle rhythms of the universe.

In the realm of personal development and self-discovery, the concept of synchronicity invites us to cultivate a deeper awareness of the interconnectedness of all things. It challenges us to relinquish our need for control and certainty, embracing instead the inherent mystery and unpredictability of life. By surrendering to the flow of synchronicity, we open ourselves to new possibilities and opportunities for growth, allowing our relationships to unfold with greater spontaneity and authenticity.

The recognition of synchronicity in relationships can have profound implications for our mental, emotional, and physical well-being. Studies have shown that individuals who report higher levels of synchronicity in their relationships tend to experience greater satisfaction, fulfillment, and overall life happiness. This correlation suggests that cultivating a receptive attitude toward synchronistic experiences may contribute to our overall sense of well-being and resilience in the face of life's challenges.

In essence, the exploration of synchronicity in relationships invites us to adopt a more expansive and inclusive view of the world, one in which every encounter, no matter how seemingly insignificant, carries the potential for profound meaning and significance. By embracing the mysteries of synchronicity, we deepen our connections with others, enrich our understanding of ourselves, and ultimately, participate more fully in the grand tapestry of existence.

As we navigate the complexities of human relationships, let us remain open to the possibility of synchronicity, trusting in the inherent wisdom and guidance of the universe. For in the dance of synchronicity, we may discover a deeper sense of purpose, belonging, and interconnectedness that transcends the limitations of our individual selves.

Exploring synchronicity in relationships prompts us to reflect on the role of intuition and inner guidance in our interactions with others. Often, synchronistic experiences are accompanied by a sense of inner knowing or resonance that transcends rational understanding. This intuitive guidance can serve as a compass, guiding us toward meaningful connections and experiences that align with our deeper purpose and intentions.

At the same time, it's important to acknowledge that not all connections are meant to be long-lasting or deeply profound. Some synchronistic encounters may serve as fleeting reminders or catalysts for growth, appearing in our lives briefly before fading away. These transient connections, though ephemeral, can still carry valuable lessons and insights if we remain open to receiving them.

Furthermore, the exploration of synchronicity invites us to reconsider the nature of time and causality in our relationships. Rather than viewing events as isolated incidents unfolding in linear succession, we come to see how past, present, and future are intertwined in a web of interconnectedness. From this perspective, every encounter holds the potential to ripple outward, influencing not only the present moment but also shaping the trajectory of our lives in unforeseen ways.

In delving deeper into the mysteries of synchronicity, we may also encounter moments of synchronistic convergence—instances where multiple threads of meaning and significance intersect in a single, synchronistic event. These moments serve as potent reminders of the interconnectedness of all things, highlighting the intricate dance of cause and effect that shapes our lives. Whether it's a chance meeting with a stranger or a serendipitous turn of events, these synchronistic convergences invite us to pause, reflect, and marvel at the profound intricacy of existence.

The exploration of synchronicity in relationships can deepen our understanding of empathy and compassion. By recognizing the interconnected nature of our experiences, we cultivate a sense of empathy for others, recognizing that their joys and sorrows are intimately intertwined with our own. This heightened sense of empathy fosters greater compassion and understanding in our interactions, paving the way for deeper and more meaningful connections with those around us.

The study of synchronicity in relationships offers a rich tapestry of insights and revelations into the interconnected nature of human experience. By embracing the mysteries of synchronicity, we expand our awareness, deepen our connections, and enrich our lives in profound and unexpected ways. As we navigate the ebb and flow of relationships, let us remain open to the synchronistic currents that flow through our lives, trusting in the wisdom and guidance of the universe to lead us toward greater understanding, fulfillment, and connection.

Furthermore, delving into the realm of synchronicity in relationships invites us to explore the role of consciousness and intentionality in shaping our interactions with others. Research in the field of quantum physics suggests that our thoughts and intentions have the power to influence the world around us, potentially giving rise to synchronistic events that align with our desires and aspirations. In this light, synchronicity becomes not merely a random occurrence, but rather a reflection of the interconnected relationship between our inner world and external reality.

The exploration of synchronicity encourages us to cultivate a sense of wonder and awe in our daily lives. By embracing the magic and mystery of synchronistic experiences, we open ourselves to a world of infinite possibilities and hidden potentials. These moments of synchronicity serve as reminders of the beauty and complexity of existence, inviting us to approach life with curiosity, gratitude, and reverence.

Additionally, the study of synchronicity in relationships can deepen our appreciation for the inherent wisdom of the universe. Synchronistic events often unfold in ways that defy logical explanation, yet carry profound meaning and significance for those involved. By surrendering to the flow of synchronicity, we acknowledge that there is a greater intelligence at work in the cosmos, guiding us toward experiences that serve our highest good and greatest growth.

Furthermore, exploring synchronicity in relationships can lead to a greater sense of interconnectedness with all of life. As we recognize the synchronistic patterns that weave through our interactions with others, we come to see how we are intimately connected to the larger web of existence. This awareness fosters a sense of unity and belonging, dissolving the illusion of separation and inviting us to embrace the interconnected tapestry of life.

The exploration of synchronicity in relationships can inspire us to cultivate a deeper sense of presence and mindfulness in our interactions with others. By paying attention to the subtle synchronistic cues that arise in our relationships, we become more attuned to the present moment, allowing us to fully engage with the richness and depth of our connections. In this way, synchronicity becomes a pathway to greater intimacy, authenticity, and mutual understanding in our relationships.

In essence, the study of synchronicity in relationships offers a gateway to a deeper understanding of ourselves, others, and the world around us. By embracing the mysteries of synchronicity, we open ourselves to new insights, experiences, and possibilities that can enrich our lives in profound and transformative ways. As we continue to explore the interconnected nature of human experience, let us remain open to the synchronistic currents that flow through our lives, guiding us toward greater wisdom, fulfillment, and connection.

Chapter 18 - Healing Synchronicities: Mind-Body Connections

In the realm of holistic healing, there exists a phenomenon that transcends conventional medical explanations and therapies: healing synchronicities. These synchronistic experiences, characterized by serendipitous events, meaningful coincidences, and spontaneous healings, highlight the profound connection between mind, body, and spirit in the healing process.

At the heart of healing synchronicities lies the idea that the body possesses an innate intelligence and capacity for self-repair that goes beyond the limits of conventional medicine. When individuals are in a state of alignment, receptivity, and openness, they may experience synchronistic events that facilitate healing on a physical, emotional, or spiritual level. These healing synchronicities often arise when individuals are willing to listen to the wisdom of their bodies, trust their intuition, and cultivate a sense of inner harmony and balance.

One common example of healing synchronicities is the phenomenon of spontaneous remission or unexpected recovery from illness or injury. These miraculous healings often occur when individuals experience a profound shift in consciousness, attitude, or belief that triggers a cascade of healing responses within the body. Whether through prayer, meditation, energy healing, or other spiritual practices, individuals may tap into a deeper wellspring of healing potential that transcends the limitations of conventional medicine.

Healing synchronicities can also manifest in the form of meaningful encounters, supportive relationships, or transformative experiences that catalyze the healing process. For example, individuals may meet a healer, mentor, or guide who provides them with the tools, insights, or resources they need to facilitate their healing journey. These synchronistic connections serve as reminders of the interconnectedness of all things and the ways in which the universe conspires to support our healing and growth.

Healing synchronicities often involve a process of inner transformation and self-discovery, as individuals confront and release old patterns, traumas, or limitations that are inhibiting their health and well-being. By listening to the messages encoded within their bodies and emotions, individuals can unlock the healing power that lies dormant within them, reclaiming their vitality, wholeness, and resilience to face life's challenges with courage and grace. This process of inner healing and self-discovery is not always easy and may require individuals to confront their deepest fears, insecurities, and wounds. By embracing the healing journey with courage and compassion, individuals can tap into their innate capacity for resilience and transformation, reclaiming their power and agency in the process. Healing synchronicities offer opportunities for individuals to reconnect with their authentic selves, aligning with their true purpose and potential in life. As they release the burdens of the past and embrace the possibilities of the present moment, individuals can experience profound shifts in consciousness and well-being, leading to greater vitality, joy, and fulfillment in all areas of their lives. Ultimately, healing synchronicities remind us that the journey of healing is not just about overcoming illness or injury, but about reclaiming our wholeness and embracing the fullness of our being.

Central to the concept of healing synchronicities is the belief in the body's inherent wisdom and its ability to self-repair beyond what traditional medicine might explain. When individuals are in tune, open, and aligned, they often encounter synchronicities that aid healing on various levels—physical, emotional, or spiritual. These instances typically arise when individuals heed their body's wisdom, trust their instincts, and cultivate inner harmony.

A prime example of healing synchronicity is the phenomenon of spontaneous remission or unanticipated recovery from illness or injury. These remarkable occurrences often stem from a profound shift in consciousness, attitude, or belief, triggering a chain reaction of healing responses within the body. Whether through practices like prayer, meditation, energy work, or other spiritual modalities, individuals tap into a wellspring of healing potential beyond conventional limits.

Healing synchronicities may also manifest as meaningful encounters, supportive relationships, or transformative experiences that accelerate the healing journey. Individuals might cross paths with a healer, mentor, or guide who equips them with the necessary tools, insights, or support to navigate their path to healing. Such synchronic connections serve as poignant reminders of the interconnectedness of all existence and the universe's propensity to aid our healing and evolution.

Furthermore, healing synchronicities often entail an inner metamorphosis and journey of self-discovery, as individuals confront and release old patterns, traumas, or limitations hindering their well-being. By attuning to their body's messages and emotional cues, individuals unlock latent healing potential, reclaiming vitality, wholeness, and resilience to confront life's trials with fortitude and grace. Although this process of inner healing and self-revelation can be challenging, embracing it with courage and compassion enables individuals to tap into their innate capacity for resilience and growth, reclaiming agency and power along the way.

These synchronicities in healing pave the way for individuals to realign with their authentic selves, embracing their true purpose and potential. Shedding the burdens of the past and embracing the present possibilities, individuals undergo profound shifts in consciousness and well-being, leading to enhanced vitality, joy, and fulfillment across all facets of life. Ultimately, healing synchronicities underscore that the journey of healing transcends mere recovery from illness or injury; it's about reclaiming wholeness and embracing the richness of our existence.

Healing synchronicities illuminate the interconnectedness between individual healing journeys and the broader cosmos. They signify a dance between the inner world of the individual and the vast tapestry of universal energies. In this intricate dance, individuals find themselves guided, supported, and sometimes gently nudged towards paths of healing and growth.

As individuals embark on their healing journeys, they often find themselves encountering synchronicities that defy logical explanation. These synchronicities serve as breadcrumbs, guiding individuals towards the next step in their evolution. Whether it's a chance encounter with a book that holds the answers they seek or a timely conversation with a stranger that offers profound insights, these synchronicities are the universe's way of communicating and nudging individuals towards alignment and wholeness.

Furthermore, healing synchronicities highlight the importance of surrender and trust in the healing process. In a world that often prioritizes control and rationality, surrendering to the flow of life can be a profound act of courage. It's about relinquishing the need to have all the answers and trusting that the universe has a plan far greater than we can comprehend. When individuals surrender to this higher intelligence, they open themselves up to a world of possibilities and synchronicities that can catalyze profound healing and transformation.

In essence, healing synchronicities are invitations to dance with the mysteries of life. They beckon individuals to step out of their comfort zones, embrace the unknown, and trust in the wisdom of the universe. It's a dance that requires courage, vulnerability, and an unwavering belief in the power of love and connection to guide us towards wholeness.

Healing synchronicities serve as reminders that healing is not a linear journey but rather a cyclical process of growth and evolution. Just as the seasons change and the tides ebb and flow, so too do our healing journeys unfold in rhythm with the natural cycles of life. There may be moments of profound breakthroughs and revelations, followed by periods of rest and integration. Each phase of the journey serves a purpose, and each synchronicity encountered along the way is a gift to be cherished and embraced.

As individuals continue to navigate their healing journeys, they may find themselves called to become agents of healing in the world. Just as they have been supported and guided by synchronicities on their own paths, they may feel compelled to pay it forward and become beacons of light and hope for others. Whether it's through sharing their stories, offering a listening ear, or simply holding space for others to heal, they become living embodiments of the healing power of synchronicity.

Healing synchronicities are profound manifestations of the interconnectedness between mind, body, spirit, and the universe. They remind us that healing is not a solitary journey but a collective dance in which we are all participants. As individuals open themselves up to the flow of synchronicity, they unlock the door to profound healing, transformation, and growth. It's a journey that requires courage, trust, and an unwavering belief in the inherent wisdom of the universe to guide us towards wholeness and alignment with our true selves.

Furthermore, healing synchronicities often lead individuals to explore modalities and practices that lie outside the realm of conventional medicine. As they open themselves up to alternative approaches such as energy healing, acupuncture, or shamanic practices, they discover new avenues for healing and transformation. These modalities tap into the body's subtle energies and the interconnected web of life, offering profound healing experiences that complement and enhance traditional medical treatments.

Besides, healing synchronicities can catalyze shifts in consciousness that ripple outwards, impacting not only the individual but also their communities and the world at large. When individuals experience profound healing and transformation, they often become catalysts for change, inspiring others to embark on their own journeys of self-discovery and growth. In this way, healing synchronicities have the power to create a ripple effect of healing and transformation that extends far beyond the individual, fostering greater harmony, compassion, and connection in the world.

Healing synchronicities invite individuals to cultivate a deeper relationship with themselves and the world around them. As they become more attuned to the subtle cues and synchronicities of life, they develop a sense of reverence and awe for the interconnected web of existence. They come to see themselves not as separate, isolated beings, but as integral parts of a larger whole, intimately connected to all of life.

Furthermore, healing synchronicities often challenge individuals to expand their understanding of what is possible and to embrace the mysteries of life with an open heart and mind. They invite individuals to surrender the need for certainty and control, and instead, to embrace the inherent uncertainty and magic of existence. In doing so, individuals open themselves up to a world of infinite possibilities, where healing can unfold in the most unexpected and miraculous ways.

Healing synchronicities are profound and mysterious phenomena that remind us of the interconnectedness of all things and the inherent wisdom of the universe. They invite us to step out of our comfort zones, embrace the unknown, and trust in the guiding hand of synchronicity to lead us towards healing and wholeness. As we open ourselves up to the flow of synchronicity, we unlock the door to profound healing, transformation, and growth, not only for ourselves but for our communities and the world at large.
Furthermore, healing synchronicities often serve as profound catalysts for personal and spiritual growth. When individuals experience synchronicities that defy rational explanation, they are prompted to question their beliefs, expand their consciousness, and explore new avenues of understanding. This journey of self-discovery leads to a deepening of their spiritual connection and a greater sense of purpose and meaning in life.

Healing synchronicities can provide individuals with a sense of hope and resilience in the face of adversity. When confronted with illness, injury, or other challenges, the experience of a synchronistic event can offer reassurance that they are not alone and that there is a larger purpose at play. This sense of connection to something greater than themselves can empower individuals to persevere through difficult times and emerge stronger and more resilient than before.

Besides, healing synchronicities can foster a profound sense of gratitude and appreciation for the beauty and wonder of life. When individuals experience synchronicities that seem to unfold with perfect timing and precision, they are reminded of the intricate and magical nature of existence. This awareness of the abundance of blessings and opportunities that surround them can cultivate a deep sense of gratitude and awe, enriching their experience of life and deepening their connection to the world around them.

Furthermore, healing synchronicities can help individuals to cultivate greater compassion and empathy for others. When individuals experience synchronicities that facilitate healing and transformation in their own lives, they are often inspired to pay it forward and support others on their healing journeys. This ripple effect of compassion and kindness can create a more caring and supportive community, where individuals come together to uplift and empower one another.

Healing synchronicities are powerful and mysterious phenomena that have the potential to profoundly transform individuals and communities alike. By opening themselves up to the flow of synchronicity and embracing the mysteries of life, individuals can unlock the door to profound healing, growth, and spiritual awakening. As they cultivate a deeper connection to themselves, to others, and to the world around them, they tap into a wellspring of resilience, hope, and compassion that empowers them to thrive in the face of life's challenges.

Healing synchronicities often spark a deepening of introspection and self-awareness. When individuals experience events that seem to align perfectly with their innermost desires or struggles, it prompts them to delve into the depths of their psyche, seeking to understand the underlying forces at play. This process of self-reflection can lead to profound insights and revelations, ultimately paving the way for personal growth and transformation.

Additionally, healing synchronicities can serve as catalysts for forgiveness and letting go of past grievances. As individuals encounter synchronistic events that bring closure or resolution to long-standing conflicts or traumas, they are presented with an opportunity to release the burdens of resentment and anger that may have weighed heavily on their hearts. In doing so, they free themselves from the shackles of the past and open themselves up to the healing power of forgiveness and reconciliation.

Furthermore, healing synchronicities can deepen individuals' connection to their intuition and inner guidance. When faced with synchronistic events that seem to offer clear signs or messages from the universe, individuals are encouraged to trust their instincts and follow the guidance of their inner voice. This heightened sense of intuition can serve as a valuable compass, guiding them towards choices and actions that are aligned with their highest good.

Healing synchronicities can inspire individuals to cultivate a greater sense of presence and mindfulness in their daily lives. As they become more attuned to the subtle synchronicities and signs that abound in the world around them, they are drawn into the richness and beauty of the present moment. This practice of mindfulness can foster a deeper appreciation for life's simple pleasures and a profound sense of peace and contentment.

Healing synchronicities are potent reminders of the interconnectedness of all things and the mysterious ways in which the universe conspires to support our healing and growth. By embracing these synchronicities with open hearts and minds, individuals can unlock the door to profound healing, transformation, and self-discovery. As they deepen their connection to themselves, to others, and to the world around them, they step into a greater sense of wholeness, vitality, and purpose in life.

Chapter 19 - The Shadow Side: Dealing with Negative Synchronistic Experiences

In the realm of synchronicity, not all experiences are uplifting or transformative. Alongside the serendipitous encounters and meaningful coincidences lie darker, more unsettling phenomena known as negative synchronistic experiences. These shadowy manifestations challenge our assumptions, shake our foundations, and confront us with the darker aspects of ourselves and the world around us.

The shadow side of synchronicity often manifests in the form of uncanny coincidences, ominous omens, or disturbing synchronistic patterns that seem to portend misfortune or calamity. Individuals may find themselves haunted by recurring themes or symbols that evoke feelings of fear, anxiety, or dread, as if they are being pursued by unseen forces beyond their control. These negative synchronistic experiences can leave individuals feeling disoriented, vulnerable, and powerless in the face of unseen threats or malevolent influences.

One common example of negative synchronistic experiences is the phenomenon of synchronistic nightmares or disturbing dreams that seem to foretell future events or symbolize unresolved fears and traumas. These unsettling dreamscapes may leave individuals feeling shaken or unsettled, as if they have glimpsed into the abyss of their own psyche and encountered hidden terrors lurking beneath the surface. While these nightmares may be deeply unsettling, they also offer opportunities for self-reflection, healing, and integration as individuals confront and process their deepest fears and anxieties.

Negative synchronistic experiences can also arise in the context of interpersonal relationships, where individuals may find themselves entangled in toxic dynamics, destructive patterns, or abusive situations that seem to defy rational explanation. Whether it's a series of unfortunate coincidences or a string of bad luck, these negative synchronistic events can take a toll on individuals' mental, emotional, and physical well-being, leaving them feeling trapped or powerless to break free from the cycle of dysfunction.

Negative synchronistic experiences can serve as wake-up calls or catalysts for personal growth and transformation, prompting individuals to confront and address the shadow aspects of themselves and their lives that they may have been avoiding or denying. By shining a light on the darker corners of the psyche, these synchronistic encounters offer opportunities for healing, integration, and reclaiming one's power and autonomy.

It's important to approach negative synchronistic experiences with caution and discernment, as they may also be indicative of underlying psychological or spiritual imbalances that require professional intervention or support. Rather than dismissing these experiences outright or succumbing to fear and paranoia, individuals can seek out resources, guidance, and assistance from qualified professionals who can help them navigate the complexities of their inner landscape.

Negative synchronistic experiences challenge us to confront the shadow aspects of ourselves and the world around us, offering opportunities for healing, growth, and transformation. By embracing these dark manifestations with courage, compassion, and self-awareness, individuals can reclaim their power and agency, transforming adversity into opportunities for self-discovery and empowerment.

The realm of negative synchronicity is fraught with eerie coincidences, foreboding omens, and disquieting patterns that seem to forewarn of impending doom or misfortune. Individuals often find themselves ensnared in a web of recurring symbols or themes that evoke feelings of apprehension, as though they are being pursued by invisible, malevolent forces beyond their comprehension. Such experiences leave them feeling adrift, vulnerable, and at the mercy of unseen influences that threaten to destabilize their lives.

One prevalent form of negative synchronistic encounters manifests in the realm of dreams—synchronistic nightmares that serve as harbingers of future events or symbolic reflections of deep-seated fears and traumas. These unsettling nocturnal visions offer a glimpse into the abyss of the subconscious, unearthing hidden anxieties and unresolved issues that plague the individual. While unsettling, these nightmares also present an opportunity for introspection, enabling individuals to confront and ultimately transcend their innermost fears.

Paradoxically, these dark encounters can also serve as catalysts for growth and self-discovery, prompting individuals to confront the shadows that lurk within and without. By illuminating the hidden recesses of the psyche, negative synchronicity offers an opportunity for healing, integration, and the reclamation of personal agency.

In essence, negative synchronistic experiences compel us to confront the darker aspects of ourselves and the world, presenting opportunities for growth, healing, and transformation. By embracing these shadowy encounters with courage and self-awareness, individuals can transcend adversity, reclaiming their power and forging a path toward self-discovery and empowerment.

Furthermore, negative synchronistic experiences serve as potent reminders of the interconnectedness between our inner worlds and external realities, highlighting the intricate dance between the conscious and unconscious realms. They beckon us to delve deeper into the depths of our psyche, exploring the uncharted territories of our fears, desires, and unresolved conflicts.

In the realm of negative synchronicity, the boundaries between the subjective and objective blur, as external events mirror internal struggles with uncanny precision. This mirroring effect challenges us to examine the role we play in shaping our experiences, inviting us to take ownership of our thoughts, emotions, and actions.

Negative synchronistic encounters often carry transformative potential, urging us to transmute fear into courage, despair into resilience, and vulnerability into strength. They compel us to embrace the darkness within, recognizing it not as a foe to be vanquished, but as a teacher guiding us toward wholeness and self-realization.

Yet, amidst the tumult of negative synchronicity, it's crucial to cultivate a sense of discernment and perspective. While these experiences may unearth buried truths and catalyze profound shifts, they can also lead us astray if we become ensnared in the labyrinth of our own fears and insecurities.

Indeed, the journey through negative synchronicity is fraught with peril, requiring us to navigate treacherous waters with steadfast resolve and unwavering clarity. It demands that we confront our deepest fears and insecurities head-on, refusing to succumb to the siren song of despair or resignation.

The path of negative synchronicity is one of profound transformation and awakening, beckoning us to transcend the limitations of our conditioning and embrace the full spectrum of human experience. It challenges us to surrender our attachments to certainty and control, embracing the inherent uncertainty and mystery of existence.

In the crucible of negative synchronicity, we are called to relinquish our illusions of separateness and recognize the interconnectedness of all things. We are reminded that every encounter, whether light or dark, carries within it the seeds of growth and evolution, propelling us ever closer to the realization of our true nature.

Negative synchronistic experiences are not merely harbingers of doom or despair but potent catalysts for personal and collective transformation. They challenge us to confront our shadow selves, embrace our vulnerabilities, and awaken to the boundless potential that lies dormant within us. As we navigate the twists and turns of this enigmatic journey, may we do so with courage, compassion, and an unwavering commitment to the light that shines within us all.

Negative synchronistic experiences beckon us to reevaluate our understanding of time and causality, inviting us to consider the possibility that the universe operates according to a deeper, more intricate order than we can fathom. They prompt us to question the linear progression of events, suggesting that past, present, and future are not separate but interconnected threads woven into the fabric of reality.

In the midst of negative synchronicity, we are confronted with the unsettling realization that the boundaries between fate and free will are more porous than we once believed. While we may strive to shape our destinies through conscious intention and action, we are also subject to forces beyond our control—forces that operate in mysterious ways, orchestrating events according to a divine or cosmic plan.

Furthermore, negative synchronistic experiences challenge us to examine the nature of belief and perception, highlighting the role that our mindset and worldview play in shaping our experiences. What we perceive as ominous or foreboding may be colored by our own fears and insecurities, reflecting back to us the shadows that dwell within our own hearts.

In this sense, negative synchronicity serves as a mirror, revealing to us the hidden aspects of ourselves that we may prefer to ignore or deny. It invites us to embrace the totality of our being—the light and the dark, the joy and the sorrow—and to recognize that within every challenge lies an opportunity for growth and self-discovery.

Negative synchronistic experiences can act as catalysts for collective awakening, stirring us from our collective slumber and prompting us to question the underlying assumptions and beliefs that govern our society. They expose the cracks in the facade of consensus reality, revealing the underlying chaos and uncertainty that lurk beneath the surface.

In the face of negative synchronicity, we are called to cultivate resilience and inner strength, recognizing that our true power lies not in avoiding adversity but in meeting it with courage and grace. It is through facing our fears and embracing the unknown that we discover the depths of our own resilience and the boundless potential that resides within us.

Negative synchronistic experiences are neither good nor bad but simply reflections of the intricate dance between the forces of light and darkness that animate the cosmos. They remind us that life is a journey of exploration and discovery, filled with twists and turns that challenge us to grow and evolve into the fullest expression of ourselves.

As we navigate the labyrinth of negative synchronicity, may we do so with open hearts and minds, embracing the lessons that each encounter has to offer. For in the darkness, we find the seeds of our greatest transformation, and in the depths of our despair, we discover the light that guides us home.

Negative synchronistic experiences also compel us to reexamine our relationship with the unseen realms and the mysterious forces that shape our lives. They challenge us to expand our awareness beyond the confines of the material world, acknowledging the existence of subtle energies and spiritual influences that may elude our rational understanding.

Negative synchronicity invites us to explore the interconnectedness between individual consciousness and the collective psyche, recognizing that our personal experiences are intricately woven into the tapestry of humanity's evolution. In this interconnected web of existence, every thought, emotion, and action reverberates across the collective consciousness, influencing the course of history in ways both subtle and profound.

In the face of negative synchronicity, we are called to cultivate a sense of humility and surrender, recognizing that there are forces at play far beyond our comprehension or control. It is through relinquishing our attachment to certainty and embracing the inherent mystery of life that we open ourselves to the possibility of profound transformation and awakening.

Furthermore, negative synchronistic experiences often serve as catalysts for spiritual emergence, propelling us into realms of consciousness beyond the confines of the egoic mind. They invite us to surrender to the flow of life, trusting in the wisdom of the universe to guide us along our journey with grace and wisdom.

In the crucible of negative synchronicity, we are invited to transcend the limitations of duality and embrace the paradoxical nature of existence. It is through embracing the darkness that we come to know the light, and through facing our fears that we discover the true depth of our courage and resilience.

Negative synchronistic experiences are invitations to embark on a journey of self-discovery and soul evolution. They beckon us to peer beyond the veil of illusion, to question the nature of reality, and to explore the infinite depths of our own being.

As we navigate the turbulent waters of negative synchronicity, may we do so with courage, compassion, and an unwavering commitment to the path of awakening. For in the heart of darkness, we find the seeds of our greatest potential, and in the depths of despair, we discover the radiant light of our true essence.

Furthermore, negative synchronistic experiences call upon us to cultivate a deeper sense of empathy and compassion, both for ourselves and for others who may be navigating similar trials. They remind us that we are not alone in our struggles, and that our shared humanity binds us together in a tapestry of interconnectedness.

In the midst of negative synchronicity, we are challenged to embrace the power of surrender—to relinquish our attachment to outcomes and trust in the unfolding of divine timing. It is through surrendering to the flow of life that we discover a profound sense of peace and acceptance, even amidst the chaos and uncertainty that may surround us.

Negative synchronistic experiences can serve as opportunities for profound healing and transformation, inviting us to release old wounds and patterns that no longer serve our highest good. They beckon us to dive deep into the recesses of our subconscious mind, where hidden traumas and limiting beliefs may lie dormant, awaiting the light of conscious awareness to set them free.

In the face of negative synchronicity, we are called to cultivate a practice of radical self-love and acceptance, embracing all aspects of ourselves—the light and the dark, the joy and the sorrow. It is through embracing our shadow selves that we come to know the fullness of our being, recognizing that every experience, no matter how challenging, holds within it the seeds of our growth and evolution.

Furthermore, negative synchronistic experiences can serve as potent reminders of the impermanent nature of existence, prompting us to cherish each moment and live fully in the present. They invite us to release our attachments to the past and future, and to embrace the richness of the present moment with gratitude and reverence.

Negative synchronicity is a sacred dance between the forces of light and dark, inviting us to navigate the terrain of our inner landscape with courage and grace. It is through facing our fears and embracing the unknown that we discover the true depth of our resilience and the boundless potential that resides within us.

As we journey through the labyrinth of negative synchronicity, may we do so with open hearts and minds, trusting in the wisdom of the universe to guide us along our path. For in the heart of darkness, we find the seeds of our greatest transformation, and in the depths of despair, we discover the radiant light of our true essence shining brightly within.

Chapter 20 - Exploring Parallel Realities: Multiverse Theory and Synchronicity

In the realm of theoretical physics, one of the most intriguing concepts is the idea of parallel realities, or the multiverse. According to this theory, our universe is just one of countless parallel universes that exist simultaneously, each with its own set of physical laws, constants, and possibilities. Within this framework, the phenomenon of synchronicity takes on new dimensions, offering insights into the interconnectedness of these parallel realities and the ways in which they intersect and influence each other.

The concept of parallel realities has its roots in quantum mechanics, the branch of physics that describes the behavior of particles at the smallest scales. According to quantum theory, particles such as electrons can exist in multiple states simultaneously, a phenomenon known as superposition. These particles can become entangled with each other, meaning that the state of one particle can instantaneously affect the state of another, regardless of the distance between them.

From this perspective, the multiverse arises as a natural consequence of quantum mechanics, with each possible outcome of a quantum event giving rise to a new branch of reality. In other words, every time a particle makes a decision, such as whether to spin up or down, the universe splits into multiple branches, each corresponding to a different outcome. This proliferation of parallel realities leads to a vast, interconnected web of possibilities, where every conceivable scenario plays out in its own universe.

Within this framework, synchronicity can be understood as the resonance between different branches of reality, where events in one universe align with events in another in meaningful and significant ways. For example, two individuals in different parallel realities may experience synchronistic events that mirror each other, such as meeting a soulmate or receiving a life-changing opportunity, despite the apparent randomness or improbability of such occurrences.

The concept of parallel realities offers a tantalizing explanation for the mysterious nature of synchronicity, suggesting that these meaningful coincidences arise from the convergence of different timelines or probability streams. In other words, synchronistic events may occur when the boundaries between parallel realities become porous or permeable, allowing for the exchange of information, energy, or consciousness between different universes.

While the idea of parallel realities may seem far-fetched or speculative, it has gained traction among physicists and cosmologists as a plausible explanation for certain phenomena, such as quantum entanglement and the fine-tuning of the laws of physics. Advances in quantum computing and experimental techniques have provided new avenues for testing and exploring the implications of multiverse theory, offering tantalizing glimpses into the hidden structure of reality.

The concept of parallel realities offers a fascinating lens through which to explore the phenomenon of synchronicity. By envisioning the universe as a vast, interconnected web of parallel universes, each with its own unique possibilities and trajectories, we gain new insights into the mysterious ways in which synchronistic events unfold. Whether viewed through the lens of quantum mechanics or philosophical speculation, the exploration of parallel realities invites us to reconsider our understanding of reality and the interconnectedness of all things.

The concept of parallel realities offers a captivating lens through which to explore the intricacies of synchronicity. By envisioning the cosmos as an interconnected tapestry of parallel universes, each branching off into its own unique trajectory, we gain fresh perspectives on the mysterious ways in which synchronous events unfold. Whether approached through the lens of quantum mechanics or philosophical inquiry, the exploration of parallel realities beckons us to reconsider our perceptions of reality and the interconnected nature of existence.

The implications of parallel realities extend beyond the realm of theoretical physics, touching upon profound philosophical and metaphysical questions about the nature of reality itself. In contemplating the existence of multiple parallel universes, we are compelled to confront fundamental inquiries about the nature of existence, consciousness, and the fabric of the cosmos.

For centuries, philosophers and mystics have pondered the interconnectedness of all things, seeking to unravel the mysteries of existence. The concept of parallel realities offers a fresh perspective on these age-old questions, suggesting that the universe is not a solitary island but rather a vast archipelago of interwoven realities, each influencing and shaping the others in profound and intricate ways.

Furthermore, the notion of parallel realities resonates deeply with certain spiritual and mystical traditions, which have long posited the existence of multiple dimensions or planes of reality beyond the material realm. In these traditions, synchronicity is often seen as a sign of alignment with higher forces or cosmic principles, signaling moments of significance and resonance between different levels of existence.

From this perspective, synchronicity becomes not merely a curious coincidence but a manifestation of the underlying unity and interconnectedness of all things. It is as if the threads of existence, woven across the vast expanse of parallel realities, occasionally converge in moments of synchronicity, reminding us of the intricate tapestry of which we are all a part.

The concept of parallel realities invites us to reconsider our notions of personal identity and agency. If there are indeed countless versions of ourselves inhabiting parallel universes, each making different choices and experiencing different outcomes, what does it mean to be "me" in the context of such a multiverse? Do we retain a core essence that transcends the boundaries of individual realities, or are we merely ephemeral manifestations of probability and chance?

These questions challenge us to expand our understanding of the self and embrace the fluidity and multiplicity of our identities across the vast expanse of parallel realities. They invite us to consider the possibility that our lives are not predetermined paths but rather branches on the tree of possibility, each leading to a different destination in the ever-expanding landscape of existence.

In exploring the concept of parallel realities and synchronicity, we are confronted with the profound mystery and wonder of existence itself. We are reminded that beneath the surface of everyday life lies a deeper reality, where the boundaries between past, present, and future blur, and the threads of possibility weave a tapestry of infinite potentiality.

The exploration of parallel realities challenges us to expand our minds and open our hearts to the boundless possibilities of existence. It beckons us to embrace the interconnectedness of all things and to recognize the subtle threads that bind us to each other and to the vast cosmic dance of which we are all a part.

In this sense, the concept of parallel realities is not merely a theoretical speculation but a profound invitation to explore the nature of reality and our place within it. It challenges us to transcend the limitations of our individual perspectives and to glimpse the underlying unity that pervades all of creation. And in doing so, it offers us a glimpse of the wondrous tapestry of existence, where synchronicity is but a thread in the rich and intricate fabric of the cosmos.

As we delve deeper into the implications of parallel realities, we encounter the notion of choice and consequence on a cosmic scale. If every decision, no matter how seemingly insignificant, spawns a new branch of reality, then the very fabric of existence becomes woven from the choices we make. This perspective imbues our actions with a profound significance, highlighting the interconnectedness of cause and effect across the multiverse.

Consider, for instance, the notion of quantum immortality, a thought experiment rooted in the concept of parallel realities. According to this idea, whenever we face a life-threatening situation, there exists a parallel reality in which we survive, no matter how improbable the outcome. From this perspective, our consciousness perpetually shifts along the branches of the multiverse, navigating a labyrinth of infinite possibilities in search of continuity and survival.

This concept challenges our conventional understanding of mortality, suggesting that death is not the end but merely a transition to another branch of reality. It prompts us to reconsider our fears and attachments in light of the vast expanse of parallel universes, where every ending is also a new beginning, and every loss is met with infinite potentiality.

Furthermore, the exploration of parallel realities invites us to contemplate the nature of time itself. If the multiverse encompasses every conceivable outcome of every quantum event, then time becomes an illusion, a mere artifact of our limited perspective. From the vantage point of parallel realities, past, present, and future are but different points along the infinite tapestry of existence, each existing simultaneously in the eternal now.

This perspective resonates with certain mystical traditions that posit a timeless, eternal reality beyond the linear progression of time. In these traditions, synchronicity is seen as a glimpse into the timeless realm of archetypal patterns and universal truths, where the past informs the present and the future beckons from beyond the horizon of our limited perception.

In essence, the concept of parallel realities challenges us to expand our understanding of reality beyond the confines of linear time and finite space. It invites us to embrace the timeless dimension of existence, where every moment is pregnant with possibility and every choice reverberates across the vast expanse of the multiverse.

The exploration of parallel realities has profound implications for our conception of free will and determinism. If every possible outcome of every choice is realized in some parallel reality, then do we truly possess free will, or are our actions predetermined by the vast web of possibilities that constitute the multiverse?

This question lies at the heart of philosophical debates about the nature of agency and responsibility in a universe governed by the principles of parallel realities. Some argue that the existence of infinite parallel universes undermines the concept of free will, reducing our choices to mere variations on predetermined outcomes. Others contend that our agency lies not in determining the outcome of events but in shaping the trajectory of our own personal narrative across the branches of the multiverse.

The concept of parallel realities opens a gateway to a realm of infinite possibility and wonder. It challenges us to transcend our limited perspective and embrace the interconnectedness of all things across the vast expanse of the multiverse. In addition, in doing so, it invites us to contemplate the nature of reality itself – a wondrous tapestry woven from the threads of possibility, where synchronicity is but a glimpse into the eternal dance of existence.

Furthermore, the concept of parallel realities prompts us to reconsider the nature of consciousness and its role in shaping the fabric of reality. If the multiverse encompasses every conceivable state of being, then consciousness becomes not merely an observer but an active participant in the creation of the cosmos. This perspective suggests that our thoughts, intentions, and beliefs have the power to shape the reality we experience, influencing the trajectory of our personal narrative across the vast expanse of parallel universes.

In exploring the interplay between consciousness and parallel realities, we encounter the notion of quantum mind, a hypothesis that posits a quantum basis for consciousness itself. According to this idea, the intricate dance of quantum particles within the brain gives rise to the phenomenon of consciousness, imbuing our subjective experience with a quantum dimension. From this perspective, the mind becomes a nexus of possibility, capable of traversing the labyrinth of parallel realities in search of meaning and understanding.

This concept challenges traditional views of consciousness as a purely biological phenomenon, suggesting that it may transcend the confines of the physical brain and extend into the vast reaches of the multiverse. It invites us to reconsider the nature of our own awareness and its relationship to the greater cosmos, opening up new avenues for exploring the mysteries of the mind and its place in the grand tapestry of existence.

The exploration of parallel realities has profound implications for our understanding of the interconnectedness of all things. If every particle in the universe is entangled with every other particle across the multiverse, then the boundaries between self and other begin to dissolve, giving rise to a sense of cosmic unity and interdependence. This perspective echoes the insights of mystics and sages throughout the ages, who have spoken of the underlying oneness of all creation.

In embracing the interconnectedness of parallel realities, we are invited to cultivate a sense of empathy and compassion for all beings, recognizing that the joys and sorrows of one are mirrored across the vast expanse of the cosmos. This realization prompts us to transcend the illusion of separation and embrace the inherent interconnectedness of all life, fostering a deeper sense of harmony and unity with the universe.

Furthermore, the concept of parallel realities challenges us to reconsider our relationship to the natural world and our role as stewards of the Earth. If every choice we make reverberates across the multiverse, then the consequences of our actions extend far beyond the boundaries of our individual lives, shaping the destiny of countless parallel worlds. This realization calls upon us to act with wisdom and compassion, recognizing the profound impact of our choices on the web of life that sustains us all.

The exploration of parallel realities invites us to embark on a journey of self-discovery and exploration, challenging us to transcend the limitations of our individual perspective and embrace the vastness of the cosmos. It beckons us to reconsider our understanding of consciousness, time, and free will, opening up new vistas of possibility and wonder. And in doing so, it invites us to glimpse the underlying unity and interconnectedness of all things, reminding us that we are but threads in the rich tapestry of existence, woven from the fabric of parallel realities.

Chapter 21 - The Quest for Meaning: Existential Perspectives on Synchronicity

In the search for meaning and purpose in life, humans have long grappled with questions of destiny, coincidence, and the mysteries of existence. At the heart of this existential quest lies the phenomenon of synchronicity, those meaningful coincidences and serendipitous encounters that seem to defy rational explanation yet carry profound significance in the lives of those who experience them. From an existential perspective, synchronicity offers insights into the nature of reality, the role of human consciousness, and the quest for meaning in an uncertain world.

Existential philosophers such as Søren Kierkegaard, Friedrich Nietzsche, and Jean-Paul Sartre have explored the complexities of human existence and the search for meaning amidst the absurdity and chaos of life. For Kierkegaard, the individual's subjective experience of reality was paramount, as each person grappled with the challenges of freedom, choice, and responsibility in the face of an indifferent universe. Nietzsche proclaimed the death of God and the need for individuals to create their own values and meaning in a world devoid of inherent purpose or morality.

From this existential perspective, synchronicity can be seen as a manifestation of the human quest for meaning and significance in a seemingly random and indifferent universe. When individuals encounter synchronistic events, they are confronted with the mystery and ambiguity of existence, prompting them to question their assumptions, beliefs, and perceptions of reality. Whether through chance encounters, meaningful coincidences, or moments of insight and revelation, synchronicity challenges individuals to confront the deeper truths and possibilities that lie beyond the surface level of everyday experience.

Synchronicity can serve as a catalyst for personal growth, transformation, and self-discovery, as individuals grapple with the existential questions and dilemmas that arise in the wake of synchronistic experiences. For example, a chance encounter with a stranger may lead to a profound conversation that sparks a new direction in life, or a serendipitous event may prompt individuals to reevaluate their priorities and values in light of newfound insights or revelations. In this way, synchronicity becomes a vehicle for existential exploration and self-transcendence, offering glimpses into the deeper dimensions of human experience and the mysteries of existence.

From a psychological perspective, existential therapy offers a framework for working with synchronicity and the existential issues it raises. By exploring the meaning and significance of synchronistic events within the context of an individual's unique life story and existential concerns, therapists can help clients navigate the existential challenges and opportunities that arise in the wake of synchronicity. Through dialogue, reflection, and exploration, individuals can cultivate a deeper understanding of themselves and their place in the world, finding meaning and purpose amidst the uncertainty and ambiguity of existence.

The quest for meaning lies at the heart of the human experience, driving us to seek understanding, purpose, and significance in a world fraught with uncertainty and complexity. From an existential perspective, synchronicity offers a window into the mysteries of existence, inviting us to explore the deeper dimensions of reality and the interconnectedness of all things. Whether viewed through the lens of philosophy, psychology, or personal experience, the quest for meaning and the phenomenon of synchronicity remind us of the profound mystery and wonder of being alive.

In humanity's relentless pursuit of purpose and significance, the enigmatic concept of synchronicity emerges as a beacon of profound exploration. At its core, synchronicity embodies those inexplicable moments of alignment, where seemingly random occurrences converge with meaning, leaving individuals grappling with the fundamental mysteries of existence. This existential odyssey delves into the very essence of reality, the intricate interplay of human consciousness, and the eternal quest for meaning amid the chaotic tapestry of life.

From this existential vantage point, synchronicity emerges as a poignant testament to humanity's relentless quest for significance in an ostensibly capricious universe. Encountering synchronistic phenomena thrusts individuals into the abyss of existential contemplation, compelling them to challenge preconceptions, unravel deeply ingrained beliefs, and reassess the very fabric of reality itself. Whether manifested through chance encounters, fortuitous coincidences, or epiphany moments of clarity, synchronicity beckons individuals to peer beyond the superficial layers of everyday existence.

Synchronicity serves as a catalyst for profound metamorphosis, ushering individuals along the path of personal growth and self-discovery. A serendipitous encounter with a stranger might unfurl into a soul-stirring dialogue, propelling one towards uncharted avenues of purpose and fulfillment. A seemingly innocuous event may unfurl a cascade of introspection, prompting individuals to reevaluate their life's trajectory and embrace newfound insights with fervor. In essence, synchronicity becomes a conduit for existential exploration, propelling individuals towards transcendence as they unearth the profound intricacies of human experience.

Within the realm of psychology, existential therapy emerges as a guiding light, offering solace amidst the tumultuous seas of synchronicity-induced existential quandaries. By unraveling the intricate tapestry of synchronistic events within the context of an individual's unique narrative, therapists weave a tapestry of understanding, aiding clients in navigating the turbulent waters of existential inquiry. Through introspective dialogue and profound introspection, individuals embark on a transformative journey towards self-realization, unraveling the enigmatic threads of their existence to unearth profound truths amidst life's nebulous uncertainties.

The eternal quest for meaning stands as humanity's quintessential pursuit, driving us towards the precipice of understanding amidst life's tumultuous currents. From an existential standpoint, synchronicity emerges as a beacon of illumination, beckoning us to explore the boundless depths of reality and the interconnectedness of all things. Whether contemplated through the lens of philosophy, dissected within the confines of psychology, or experienced firsthand in the tapestry of life, synchronicity serves as a poignant reminder of the ineffable mystery and wonder that permeate the fabric of existence.

In the ceaseless quest for meaning and significance, humanity finds itself ensnared in the labyrinth of existential inquiry, grappling with the complexities of destiny, chance, and the profound enigma of existence itself. Synchronicity, with its elusive dance of meaningful coincidences and fortuitous encounters, emerges as a tantalizing enigma at the heart of this existential odyssey. It transcends the boundaries of rational explanation, beckoning individuals to delve deeper into the recesses of their consciousness and confront the enigmatic tapestry of life's interconnectedness.

Across the annals of philosophical discourse, luminaries such as Søren Kierkegaard, Friedrich Nietzsche, and Jean-Paul Sartre have tirelessly plumbed the depths of human consciousness, probing the intricacies of existence in search of meaning amidst the chaotic expanse of the universe. Kierkegaard's emphasis on subjective truth, Nietzsche's proclamation of the "will to power," and Sartre's existential anguish all converge upon the central theme of human agency and the relentless pursuit of authenticity in a world fraught with ambiguity.

In essence, synchronicity serves as a mirror reflecting the existential dilemmas and paradoxes that permeate the human condition. When individuals encounter synchronistic events, they are confronted with a stark reminder of the interconnectedness of all things, prompting them to reassess their place within the grand tapestry of existence. These encounters often serve as catalysts for introspection and self-examination, inviting individuals to explore the deeper recesses of their psyche and confront the existential truths that lie beyond the veil of mundane reality.

Furthermore, synchronicity transcends the realm of mere happenstance, often serving as a harbinger of profound transformation and personal growth. Through synchronistic encounters, individuals are presented with opportunities to break free from the shackles of routine and convention, embarking on a journey of self-discovery and self-actualization. Whether through chance meetings, unexpected revelations, or serendipitous insights, synchronicity propels individuals towards the precipice of self-transcendence, inviting them to embrace the fullness of their existence with renewed vigor and purpose.

From a psychological standpoint, existential therapy provides a fertile ground for exploring the existential implications of synchronicity and its profound impact on the human psyche. Therapists adept in existential principles guide individuals through the labyrinth of existential angst, helping them navigate the murky waters of uncertainty and ambiguity that often accompany synchronistic experiences. Through dialogue, introspection, and existential inquiry, individuals gain a deeper understanding of themselves and their place within the cosmic dance of existence, finding solace amidst life's inherent unpredictability.

The phenomenon of synchronicity stands as a testament to the profound interconnectedness of all things, inviting humanity to peer beyond the veil of superficial reality and explore the deeper mysteries that lie beneath. From the existential musings of philosophers to the therapeutic insights of psychologists, synchronicity serves as a potent reminder of the ineffable beauty and complexity of the human experience. As we navigate the tumultuous seas of existence, let us embrace synchronicity as a guiding light, illuminating the path towards self-discovery, transformation, and ultimately, the realization of our truest selves within the vast expanse of the universe.

The allure of synchronicity extends beyond individual introspection, permeating the very fabric of human society and culture. Throughout history, synchronistic events have woven themselves into the collective consciousness of communities, shaping cultural narratives, and imbuing collective experiences with profound meaning and significance. From ancient myths and religious texts to modern-day folklore and urban legends, synchronicity serves as a recurring motif, reminding humanity of the interconnectedness of all things and the inherent mystery that pervades the human experience.

In the realm of art and creativity, synchronicity emerges as a muse, inspiring artists, writers, and visionaries to tap into the wellspring of collective consciousness and channel the ineffable currents of inspiration. Countless works of literature, music, and visual art bear the imprint of synchronistic encounters, serving as poignant reminders of the transformative power of serendipity and chance in the creative process. From the chance meeting that sparks a lifelong collaboration to the fortuitous discovery that ignites a revolution in artistic expression, synchronicity infuses the creative landscape with a sense of magic and wonder, inviting creators to embrace the serendipitous dance of inspiration and intuition.

Furthermore, the exploration of synchronicity transcends the confines of individual experience, extending into the realms of science and quantum physics. While traditionally viewed as a phenomenon outside the purview of empirical inquiry, synchronicity has garnered the attention of pioneering scientists and researchers seeking to unravel its enigmatic nature. Within the framework of quantum mechanics, the notion of non-locality and entanglement offers tantalizing insights into the interconnected nature of reality, suggesting that synchronicity may arise from deeper quantum phenomena that transcend our conventional understanding of causality and determinism.

In the quest to unravel the mysteries of synchronicity, interdisciplinary approaches offer a promising avenue for exploration, bridging the gap between subjective experience and objective inquiry. By integrating insights from philosophy, psychology, art, and science, scholars and researchers can gain a more comprehensive understanding of synchronicity and its implications for our understanding of consciousness, reality, and the nature of existence itself. Through collaborative efforts and interdisciplinary dialogue, humanity stands poised to unlock the secrets of synchronicity and harness its transformative potential for the betterment of individuals and society as a whole.

The phenomenon of synchronicity serves as a profound reminder of the interconnectedness of all things and the inherent mystery that lies at the heart of the human experience. Whether contemplated through the lens of philosophy, explored through the realms of psychology and therapy, or studied within the frameworks of science and quantum physics, synchronicity invites humanity to embrace the enigmatic dance of existence with open hearts and curious minds. As we navigate the labyrinth of life, let us heed the call of synchronicity, embracing the serendipitous encounters and meaningful coincidences that illuminate our path and enrich our journey through the vast expanse of the cosmos.

The exploration of synchronicity invites us to reconsider our relationship with time and causality, challenging conventional notions of linear progression and deterministic outcomes. From the perspective of synchronicity, time unfolds not as a linear procession of events but as a multidimensional tapestry where past, present, and future converge in a kaleidoscopic dance of interconnectedness. In this paradigm, meaningful coincidences serve as nodal points, linking disparate moments across the temporal continuum and offering glimpses into the underlying unity of all existence.

As humanity delves deeper into the mysteries of synchronicity, the implications for our understanding of consciousness and the nature of reality become increasingly profound. Within the framework of synchronicity, consciousness emerges not as a localized phenomenon confined to individual minds but as a vast, interconnected web that permeates the fabric of the cosmos. In this holistic perspective, every thought, emotion, and intention ripples outward, shaping the contours of reality and giving rise to the synchronistic dance of meaningful coincidences that punctuate our lives.

Furthermore, the study of synchronicity beckons us to reconsider the role of intentionality and agency in shaping our lived experience. While traditional notions of causality posit a linear relationship between cause and effect, synchronicity suggests a more nuanced interplay between intentionality and receptivity, wherein our conscious desires intersect with the deeper currents of the collective unconscious to manifest meaningful coincidences in our lives. By cultivating a state of open receptivity and aligning our intentions with the greater flow of life, we may enhance our capacity to attract synchronistic events and harness their transformative potential for personal growth and self-realization.

In the realm of spirituality and mysticism, synchronicity emerges as a gateway to higher states of consciousness and expanded awareness. Across diverse spiritual traditions, synchronistic events are often interpreted as divine messages or signs from the universe, guiding individuals along the path of spiritual awakening and enlightenment. Whether viewed through the lens of Eastern mysticism, Western esotericism, or indigenous wisdom traditions, synchronicity serves as a potent reminder of our interconnectedness with the cosmos and our inherent capacity to co-create our reality in harmony with the greater intelligence that animates all of creation.

The phenomenon of synchronicity beckons us to transcend the limitations of linear thinking and embrace the boundless possibilities of a universe infused with meaning and purpose. As we navigate the labyrinth of existence, let us heed the call of synchronicity, opening ourselves to the profound mysteries that lie beyond the veil of ordinary perception. In doing so, we may unlock the transformative power of synchronicity and embark on a journey of self-discovery, spiritual awakening, and cosmic exploration that transcends the boundaries of time and space.

Chapter 22 - The Synchronistic Universe: Finding Order in Chaos

Amidst the apparent chaos and randomness of the universe, there exists a subtle yet profound order that reveals itself through the phenomenon of synchronicity. From the intricate dance of celestial bodies to the serendipitous encounters of everyday life, synchronicity invites us to glimpse the underlying harmony and interconnectedness that permeate the fabric of reality. In exploring the synchronistic universe, we embark on a journey of discovery, seeking to uncover the hidden patterns and meanings that lie beneath the surface of existence.

At its core, the synchronistic universe challenges our conventional notions of causality and determinism, suggesting that meaningful coincidences and serendipitous events arise from a deeper, more fundamental source of order and intelligence. Rather than being purely random or arbitrary, synchronistic experiences reflect the interconnectedness of all things and the ways in which the universe conspires to guide, support, and awaken us to new possibilities.

One of the key insights of the synchronistic universe is the idea that time is not linear but rather a multidimensional tapestry in which past, present, and future coexist simultaneously. From this perspective, synchronicity arises when events in different temporal dimensions intersect and align in meaningful and significant ways. For example, a dream may foreshadow a future event, or a chance encounter may resonate with a past experience, suggesting that time is not an immutable arrow but rather a fluid and dynamic continuum.

The synchronistic universe invites us to reconsider our understanding of consciousness and the role it plays in shaping our perceptions of reality. From the perspective of synchronicity, consciousness is not confined to the individual mind but rather an intrinsic aspect of the fabric of reality itself. In other words, consciousness pervades all levels of existence, from the subatomic realm to the cosmic scale, weaving a tapestry of interconnectedness and meaning that transcends the limitations of the individual ego.

From a scientific perspective, the synchronistic universe finds resonance in the emerging field of complexity theory, which explores the behavior of complex systems and the emergence of order from chaos. Complex systems, such as the weather, ecosystems, or the human brain, exhibit nonlinear dynamics that give rise to self-organizing patterns and phenomena. Within this framework, synchronicity can be seen as a manifestation of the inherent order and intelligence of complex systems, where seemingly disparate elements converge to create moments of significance and resonance.

Besides its scientific implications, the synchronistic universe also has profound philosophical and spiritual significance. It invites us to contemplate the nature of reality and our place within it, challenging us to expand our awareness and embrace the interconnectedness of all things. By recognizing and honoring the synchronistic cues present in our lives, we can cultivate a deeper sense of meaning, purpose, and connection, leading to greater fulfillment and harmony in our relationships, our work, and our journey through life.

The synchronistic universe offers a rich tapestry of insights into the nature of reality and the mysteries of existence. By exploring the interconnectedness of all things and the profound order that underlies the apparent chaos of the universe, we can uncover new pathways to understanding, growth, and transformation. Whether viewed through the lens of science, philosophy, or personal experience, the synchronistic universe reminds us of the inherent beauty and intelligence of the cosmos, inviting us to embrace the mystery and wonder of being alive.

Amidst the seemingly chaotic dance of the cosmos, there exists an intricate order that unveils itself through the concept of synchronicity. This subtle yet profound phenomenon invites us to glimpse the interconnected harmony woven into the fabric of reality, from the grand movements of celestial bodies to the chance encounters of everyday life. Delving into the synchronistic universe propels us on a journey of exploration, as we seek to unravel the concealed patterns and meanings hidden beneath the surface of existence.

At its essence, the synchronistic universe challenges the conventional understanding of causality and determinism. It proposes that meaningful coincidences and serendipitous events stem from a deeper, more fundamental source of order and intelligence. Rather than mere chance occurrences, synchronistic experiences mirror the interconnectedness of all things, illustrating how the universe conspires to guide, support, and awaken us to fresh possibilities.

Central to the concept of the synchronistic universe is the notion that time transcends linearity, existing as a multidimensional tapestry where past, present, and future coalesce simultaneously. This perspective suggests that synchronicity occurs when events from different temporal dimensions intersect and harmonize in meaningful ways. For instance, a dream may foretell a forthcoming event, or a spontaneous encounter may resonate with a past experience, indicating that time flows as a fluid continuum rather than a rigid arrow.

Furthermore, the synchronistic universe prompts a reevaluation of consciousness and its role in shaping our perceptions of reality. Rather than being confined to individual minds, consciousness is viewed as an inherent aspect of reality itself. It permeates all levels of existence, from the minuscule realms of subatomic particles to the vast expanses of the cosmos, weaving a tapestry of interconnectedness and significance that surpasses the boundaries of the ego.

Beyond its scientific implications, the synchronistic universe holds profound philosophical and spiritual significance. It beckons us to contemplate the nature of reality and our position within it, urging us to expand our awareness and embrace the interconnectedness of existence. By acknowledging and honoring the synchronistic signals present in our lives, we can cultivate a deeper sense of purpose, meaning, and connection. This, in turn, fosters greater fulfillment and harmony in our relationships, endeavors, and passage through life.

The synchronistic universe presents a multifaceted tapestry of insights into the nature of reality and the enigmas of existence. By delving into the interconnectedness of all things and the inherent order underlying the apparent chaos of the universe, we unveil new avenues to comprehension, growth, and metamorphosis. Whether through the lens of science, philosophy, or personal experience, the synchronistic universe serves as a reminder of the intrinsic beauty and intelligence pervading the cosmos. It invites us to embrace the mystery and marvel of being alive, fostering a deeper appreciation for the intricate dance of existence.

Expanding upon the profound implications of the synchronistic universe, we find ourselves drawn into a deeper exploration of its implications for our understanding of reality. Through synchronicity, we are presented with a lens through which to view the interconnectedness of all phenomena, transcending the limitations of traditional linear causality. This perspective challenges us to reconsider our perceptions of the universe as a mere collection of isolated events, instead inviting us to recognize the intricate web of relationships that underlies every aspect of existence.

In delving into the depths of the synchronistic universe, we encounter the concept of resonance – the idea that certain events, experiences, or encounters carry a unique vibrational frequency that resonates with our own consciousness. These moments of resonance serve as signposts along our journey, guiding us towards deeper understanding and self-discovery. Whether it be a chance encounter with a kindred spirit or a serendipitous revelation that illuminates our path, these synchronistic moments have the power to catalyze profound shifts in our awareness and perception.

The synchronistic universe invites us to consider the role of intentionality in shaping our reality. Rather than passive observers in the unfolding drama of existence, we are active participants, co-creators of our own destinies. Through the power of intention and mindfulness, we have the ability to align ourselves with the underlying currents of synchronicity, thereby opening ourselves to a greater flow of abundance, opportunity, and synchronistic encounters.

At its core, the synchronistic universe challenges us to embrace uncertainty and ambiguity, recognizing that within the chaos lies the potential for profound insight and revelation. It invites us to cultivate a sense of openness and receptivity to the unexpected, trusting in the inherent wisdom of the universe to guide us along our path. In doing so, we learn to surrender our attachment to rigid notions of control and certainty, embracing instead the fluidity and spontaneity of the synchronistic dance.

In the realm of personal transformation, the synchronistic universe serves as a catalyst for growth and evolution. Through the recognition and integration of synchronistic experiences into our lives, we gain a deeper understanding of ourselves and our place within the larger tapestry of existence. These moments of synchronicity act as mirrors, reflecting back to us aspects of our own consciousness that may have previously lain dormant or unrecognized. In this way, synchronicity becomes a powerful tool for self-discovery and self-realization, leading us towards greater wholeness and authenticity.

From a societal perspective, the implications of the synchronistic universe are equally profound. As we awaken to the interconnectedness of all beings and the interdependence of all life forms, we are called to cultivate a greater sense of compassion, empathy, and stewardship towards the planet and its inhabitants. The recognition of synchronicity reminds us that every action we take, no matter how seemingly insignificant, has ripple effects that reverberate throughout the web of existence. In this way, synchronicity becomes a guiding principle for social and environmental activism, inspiring us to work towards a more just, equitable, and sustainable world for future generations.

The synchronistic universe offers us a profound invitation to explore the hidden depths of reality and uncover the interconnectedness that lies at its core. Through synchronicity, we are reminded of the inherent order and intelligence that pervade the cosmos, inviting us to embrace the mystery and wonder of existence. Whether viewed through the lens of science, spirituality, or personal experience, the synchronistic universe offers us a glimpse into the infinite possibilities that lie beyond the veil of ordinary perception. It is a reminder that we are part of something far greater than ourselves, and that the journey of discovery is as infinite and boundless as the universe itself.

In our exploration of the synchronistic universe, we find ourselves delving deeper into the profound implications of synchronicity for our understanding of consciousness and reality. At its essence, synchronicity challenges us to reevaluate our perception of time as a linear progression and instead consider it as a multidimensional fabric where past, present, and future coalesce in a timeless dance. This perspective suggests that every moment is pregnant with infinite potential, with past events influencing the present and the future unfolding in a dynamic interplay of possibilities.

Within the framework of the synchronistic universe, consciousness emerges as a fundamental aspect of reality, intimately interconnected with the fabric of existence itself. Rather than viewing consciousness as a byproduct of brain activity confined to individual minds, synchronicity invites us to recognize it as a universal force that permeates all levels of reality. From the subatomic particles that form the building blocks of matter to the vast expanse of cosmic consciousness, every facet of existence is imbued with the spark of awareness, weaving a tapestry of interconnectedness that transcends the limitations of the ego.

In exploring the scientific underpinnings of synchronicity, we find resonance with the principles of quantum mechanics and complexity theory. Quantum mechanics, with its emphasis on the interconnected nature of particles and the role of observation in shaping reality, provides a theoretical framework for understanding the nonlocality and entanglement inherent in synchronistic phenomena. Complexity theory offers insights into the emergent properties of complex systems, where seemingly disparate elements interact to give rise to higher-order patterns and behaviors. Within this context, synchronicity can be seen as a manifestation of the self-organizing dynamics that underlie the universe, where events coalesce in meaningful ways to form patterns of significance and resonance.

The study of synchronicity has profound implications for our understanding of human psychology and consciousness. Carl Jung, the pioneering psychologist who first coined the term "synchronicity," recognized the importance of synchronistic experiences in the process of individuation – the journey towards wholeness and self-realization. According to Jung, synchronicity serves as a bridge between the conscious and unconscious realms of the psyche, offering insights into the deeper layers of the unconscious mind and guiding us towards greater self-awareness and integration.

From a spiritual perspective, the synchronistic universe invites us to explore the nature of our connection to the divine and the mysteries of existence. Whether viewed through the lens of Eastern mysticism, Western esoteric traditions, or indigenous cosmologies, synchronicity is seen as a reflection of the underlying unity and interconnectedness of all things. It is a reminder that we are not separate from the cosmos but rather an integral part of its vast and intricate tapestry, each of us playing a unique role in the unfolding drama of creation.

The synchronistic universe offers us a profound glimpse into the hidden dimensions of reality and the mysteries of existence. Through synchronicity, we are invited to explore the interconnectedness of all things and the underlying order that governs the cosmos. Whether through scientific inquiry, psychological introspection, or spiritual revelation, the study of synchronicity opens doors to new realms of understanding and insight. It is a reminder that we are not mere observers of the universe but active participants in its ongoing evolution, co-creators of our own destinies in a cosmic dance of synchronicity and meaning.

Chapter 23 - Practical Applications: Harnessing Synchronicity for Personal Growth

Synchronicity, with its mysterious and often profound nature, isn't just a curious phenomenon to marvel at—it can also serve as a powerful tool for personal growth and self-discovery. By understanding and harnessing the principles of synchronicity, individuals can unlock new pathways to insight, inspiration, and transformation in their lives.

One practical application of synchronicity is in the realm of manifestation and goal-setting. Rather than relying solely on sheer willpower or effort to achieve their goals, individuals can learn to align themselves with the flow of synchronistic events and opportunities that arise naturally in their lives. By cultivating a sense of openness, receptivity, and trust, individuals can create fertile ground for synchronicity to flourish, leading to unexpected breakthroughs, creative solutions, and serendipitous encounters that support their goals and aspirations.

Synchronicity can also be used as a tool for self-reflection and introspection. When individuals encounter synchronistic events, they are invited to pause and reflect on the deeper meaning and significance behind these experiences. By journaling, meditating, or engaging in dialogue with others, individuals can gain insights into the underlying patterns, themes, and messages that emerge through synchronicity, leading to greater clarity, insight, and self-awareness.

Another practical application of synchronicity is in the realm of decision-making and problem-solving. When faced with important choices or challenges, individuals can learn to pay attention to the synchronistic cues and clues that arise in their lives, guiding them towards the most aligned and beneficial course of action. By trusting their intuition, following their inner guidance, and remaining open to unexpected opportunities, individuals can navigate life's twists and turns with greater ease, confidence, and grace.

Furthermore, synchronicity can also be used as a tool for fostering deeper connections and relationships with others. When individuals recognize and honor the synchronistic connections that exist between themselves and others, they can cultivate more meaningful and authentic relationships built on trust, empathy, and mutual understanding. By acknowledging the role that synchronicity plays in bringing people together, individuals can deepen their sense of belonging, community, and shared purpose in the world.

The practical applications of synchronicity are vast and varied, offering individuals new ways to navigate life's challenges, pursue their goals, and deepen their connections with themselves and others. By harnessing the power of synchronicity, individuals can unlock new pathways to insight, inspiration, and growth, leading to greater fulfillment, joy, and alignment in every aspect of their lives.

Synchronicity, with its enigmatic and often profound essence, transcends mere curiosity—it becomes a potent catalyst for personal evolution and self-realization. Delving into the intricacies of synchronicity unveils a realm where individuals can embark on transformative journeys, unlocking vistas of insight, inspiration, and growth.

An intriguing avenue where synchronicity manifests its influence is in the domain of manifestation and goal attainment. Rather than relying solely on brute force or relentless effort to materialize their aspirations, individuals can learn the art of synchronistic alignment. Cultivating traits of openness, receptivity, and trust sets the stage for synchronicity to weave its magic, ushering in unforeseen breakthroughs, ingenious solutions, and fortuitous encounters that propel individuals toward their objectives.

Furthermore, synchronicity serves as a mirror for self-examination and introspection. When synchronistic occurrences grace an individual's path, they beckon pause and reflection upon the deeper layers of meaning they carry. Through practices like journaling, meditation, or meaningful dialogue, individuals unravel the underlying tapestry of patterns, themes, and messages woven by synchronicity, fostering enhanced clarity, profound insights, and heightened self-awareness.

Another realm where synchronicity manifests its utility is in the arena of decision-making and problem-solving. Confronted with pivotal choices or hurdles, individuals attuned to synchronistic nuances discern cues and hints guiding them toward optimal courses of action. Trusting intuition, heeding inner guidance, and embracing unexpected opportunities enable individuals to navigate life's complexities with poise, assurance, and grace.

Synchronicity becomes a conduit for forging deeper bonds and connections with fellow beings. Acknowledging and cherishing the synchronistic threads intertwining individuals fosters richer, more authentic relationships anchored in trust, empathy, and mutual resonance. Recognizing synchronicity's role in fostering connections cultivates a profound sense of belonging, community, and shared purpose.

In summary, the practical implications of synchronicity are manifold, offering individuals novel avenues to traverse life's terrain, pursue aspirations, and deepen connections both within and without. By harnessing the inherent power of synchronicity, individuals embark on transformative odysseys, unveiling realms of insight, inspiration, and growth, ultimately culminating in profound fulfillment, boundless joy, and harmonious alignment across all facets of existence.

Expanding upon the multifaceted realm of synchronicity reveals its profound implications across various dimensions of human experience. One such dimension lies in the realm of creativity and innovation. Synchronicity, with its inherent capacity to orchestrate seemingly unrelated events and ideas, serves as a fertile ground for creative breakthroughs and innovative insights. By embracing synchronistic occurrences with an open mind and receptive spirit, individuals can tap into a reservoir of inspiration, leading to novel solutions, artistic expressions, and inventive endeavors.

Furthermore, the realm of synchronicity extends its influence into the realm of healing and well-being. As individuals attune themselves to the synchronistic rhythms of life, they often find themselves guided towards experiences, practices, and resources that support their physical, emotional, and spiritual well-being. Whether it be stumbling upon a timely piece of advice, encountering a supportive community, or experiencing moments of profound serenity, synchronicity plays a pivotal role in facilitating holistic healing and inner transformation.

The phenomenon of synchronicity underscores the interconnectedness of all beings and the universe at large. Each synchronistic encounter serves as a reminder of the intricate web of existence in which we are all enmeshed. By recognizing the interplay of cause and effect, intention and manifestation, individuals gain a deeper appreciation for the profound interconnectedness of life, fostering a sense of reverence, gratitude, and awe for the mysteries of existence.

Besides, the realm of synchronicity invites individuals to cultivate a sense of synchronistic living—an approach to life characterized by attunement to the flow of synchronistic events and the subtle guidance of intuition. As individuals align themselves with the natural rhythms of life, they find themselves in a state of flow, where opportunities unfold effortlessly, obstacles dissolve, and serendipitous encounters abound. Synchronistic living thus becomes a pathway to greater harmony, abundance, and fulfillment, as individuals navigate the currents of life with grace and ease.

Furthermore, the exploration of synchronicity invites individuals to transcend the limitations of linear thinking and rationality, embracing a more expansive and holistic worldview. In a world where logic and reason often reign supreme, synchronicity reminds us of the inherent mystery and magic that permeate the fabric of reality. By embracing the paradoxes, uncertainties, and synchronistic surprises that life has to offer, individuals embark on a journey of self-discovery and spiritual awakening, transcending the confines of the ego and opening themselves to the boundless possibilities of the universe.

In essence, the phenomenon of synchronicity transcends mere coincidence, offering a profound glimpse into the underlying order and intelligence that governs the universe. As individuals awaken to the synchronistic dance of life, they unlock new pathways to creativity, healing, connection, and self-realization. In embracing the mysteries of synchronicity, individuals embark on a journey of profound transformation, unfolding the hidden dimensions of their being and aligning themselves with the infinite possibilities of existence.

The exploration of synchronicity delves into the realm of spirituality and transcendence. Synchronistic experiences often evoke a sense of awe and wonder, inviting individuals to contemplate the deeper mysteries of existence and their place within the cosmic tapestry. Through practices such as meditation, prayer, and contemplation, individuals can cultivate a deeper connection to the divine or the universal consciousness from which synchronicity emerges. This spiritual dimension of synchronicity offers a profound sense of meaning, purpose, and connection, guiding individuals on a journey of inner exploration and self-realization.

Additionally, synchronicity can serve as a catalyst for collective evolution and societal transformation. When synchronistic events occur on a larger scale, they have the potential to catalyze shifts in collective consciousness and social dynamics. Whether it be the emergence of a transformative idea, the spontaneous convergence of like-minded individuals, or the synchronistic timing of cultural movements, synchronicity can play a pivotal role in shaping the course of human history. By recognizing and harnessing the power of synchronicity in collective endeavors, humanity can move towards a more harmonious, equitable, and sustainable future.

Furthermore, the study of synchronicity invites individuals to explore the intersection of science and spirituality. While synchronicity may defy conventional scientific explanation, it offers a fertile ground for interdisciplinary inquiry and exploration. Quantum physics, complexity theory, and consciousness studies provide frameworks through which synchronicity can be understood as a fundamental aspect of reality. By bridging the gap between science and spirituality, individuals can gain a deeper understanding of the interconnected nature of existence and the profound implications of synchronicity for our understanding of the universe.

The integration of synchronicity into everyday life requires a willingness to surrender to the unknown and embrace the unfolding mystery of existence. In a world characterized by uncertainty and change, synchronicity offers a guiding light amidst the chaos, reminding individuals to trust in the inherent wisdom of the universe. By relinquishing the need for control and allowing synchronicity to guide their journey, individuals can experience a profound sense of liberation and empowerment, as they surrender to the flow of life and embrace the magic of synchronicity.

The exploration of synchronicity reveals it to be a phenomenon of profound significance with far-reaching implications for personal growth, collective evolution, and our understanding of the nature of reality. By embracing synchronicity as a guiding principle in our lives, we open ourselves to new possibilities, deeper connections, and a greater sense of meaning and purpose. In the dance of synchronicity, we discover a profound truth—that we are not separate, isolated beings, but interconnected threads woven into the rich tapestry of existence, where every moment is imbued with meaning and significance.

Furthermore, the concept of synchronicity invites exploration into the nature of time and causality. In synchronistic experiences, the linear constraints of time seem to dissolve, giving rise to a sense of timelessness and interconnectedness. Events that occur seemingly unrelated in linear time reveal hidden connections and patterns when viewed through the lens of synchronicity. This challenges traditional notions of cause and effect, suggesting a deeper underlying order to the unfolding of events in the universe. By embracing the nonlinear nature of synchronicity, individuals can transcend the limitations of linear thinking and expand their understanding of the interconnectedness of past, present, and future.

The practice of cultivating synchronicity in daily life requires a state of heightened awareness and mindfulness. By cultivating present moment awareness and attuning to the subtle cues and signals of synchronicity, individuals can enhance their ability to recognize and respond to synchronistic events as they arise. This mindfulness practice fosters a deeper connection to the underlying rhythms of life, enabling individuals to navigate the ebb and flow of synchronicity with greater ease and grace.

Additionally, the exploration of synchronicity invites individuals to explore the role of intention and alignment in shaping their experiences. Synchronistic events often seem to unfold in response to individuals' intentions, desires, and energetic vibrations. By aligning their thoughts, feelings, and actions with their highest aspirations and values, individuals can magnetize synchronistic opportunities and experiences into their lives. This process of intentional alignment empowers individuals to co-create their reality in partnership with the synchronistic forces of the universe.

Furthermore, the study of synchronicity opens doors to new ways of perceiving and interacting with the world around us. By embracing a paradigm shift from a mechanistic, deterministic worldview to one that honors the mystery and interconnectedness of all things, individuals can cultivate a deeper sense of reverence and appreciation for the beauty and complexity of existence. This shift in perspective invites individuals to approach life with a sense of wonder, curiosity, and awe, fostering a profound sense of connection and belonging to the greater web of life.

In essence, the exploration of synchronicity unveils a rich tapestry of insights, experiences, and possibilities that transcend the boundaries of conventional understanding. By delving into the mysteries of synchronicity, individuals embark on a journey of self-discovery, spiritual awakening, and collective evolution. In embracing the magic and wonder of synchronicity, we open ourselves to a world of infinite potential and possibility, where every moment is imbued with meaning, significance, and the promise of new beginnings.

The phenomenon of synchronicity challenges individuals to cultivate a sense of trust and surrender in the face of uncertainty. In a world characterized by constant change and unpredictability, embracing synchronicity requires letting go of the need for rigid control and allowing life to unfold organically. This surrender to the flow of synchronicity does not imply passivity or resignation but rather an active engagement with the present moment, trusting that the universe is guiding us towards our highest good. By relinquishing attachment to specific outcomes and remaining open to the infinite possibilities of synchronicity, individuals can navigate life's twists and turns with greater resilience, grace, and peace of mind.

Additionally, the exploration of synchronicity encourages individuals to cultivate practices that enhance their receptivity to synchronistic experiences. Meditation, mindfulness, and contemplative practices serve as powerful tools for quieting the mind, opening the heart, and attuning to the subtle energies of synchronicity. By creating space for stillness and silence in their lives, individuals can deepen their connection to their intuition and inner guidance, allowing synchronicity to flow more freely into their awareness. This practice of inner listening and receptivity enables individuals to align more fully with the synchronistic currents of life, facilitating greater harmony, flow, and alignment with their true purpose and potential.

Furthermore, the phenomenon of synchronicity invites individuals to explore the interconnected nature of reality and the web of relationships that bind us together. Every synchronistic encounter, whether with another person, a place, or a moment in time, is a reminder of our interconnectedness and interdependence with all beings and phenomena. By honoring the synchronistic connections that weave through our lives, individuals can cultivate a deeper sense of empathy, compassion, and solidarity with others, fostering greater harmony and cooperation in our relationships and communities. This recognition of our shared humanity and interconnectedness lies at the heart of a more just, equitable, and compassionate world.

The study of synchronicity encourages individuals to embrace the mystery and magic of life with a sense of wonder and curiosity. Rather than seeking to analyze or rationalize synchronistic experiences, individuals are invited to approach them with an attitude of openness and receptivity, allowing the beauty and mystery of synchronicity to unfold naturally. By embracing the paradoxes, uncertainties, and synchronistic surprises that life presents, individuals can awaken to the profound mysteries of existence and cultivate a deeper appreciation for the miraculous nature of reality. This sense of awe and wonder serves as a catalyst for personal growth, spiritual awakening, and the expansion of consciousness.

The exploration of synchronicity opens doorways to new realms of understanding, insight, and possibility. By embracing the magic and mystery of synchronicity, individuals can awaken to the interconnectedness of all things and cultivate a deeper sense of meaning, purpose, and connection in their lives. As we surrender to the flow of synchronicity, we embark on a journey of self-discovery, spiritual awakening, and collective evolution, guided by the wisdom and intelligence of the universe. In embracing synchronicity, we step into the fullness of our being and the boundless potential of existence, where every moment is infused with meaning, significance, and the promise of transformation.

Chapter 24 - Conclusion: Embracing the Mystery of Synchronicity

In the grand tapestry of existence, there exists a phenomenon that transcends logic, reason, and scientific explanation: synchronicity. From the seemingly random encounters of everyday life to the profound insights and revelations that shape our destinies, synchronicity invites us to embrace the mystery and wonder of the universe in all its complexity and beauty.

At its core, synchronicity challenges us to expand our awareness and perception of reality, inviting us to see beyond the limitations of the rational mind and into the deeper dimensions of existence. Rather than viewing the world as a collection of isolated events and random occurrences, synchronicity reveals the interconnectedness and interdependence of all things, weaving a tapestry of meaning and significance that extends far beyond our ordinary understanding.

Synchronicity serves as a reminder of the inherent intelligence and creativity of the universe, inviting us to trust in the unseen forces and patterns that guide and shape our lives. Whether viewed through the lens of science, spirituality, or personal experience, synchronicity offers a glimpse into the underlying harmony and order that underlies the apparent chaos and randomness of the world.

In embracing the mystery of synchronicity, we open ourselves to new possibilities, insights, and opportunities for growth and transformation. By cultivating a sense of openness, receptivity, and trust, we can harness the power of synchronicity to navigate life's challenges, pursue our goals, and deepen our connections with ourselves and others.

Synchronicity invites us to embrace the beauty and wonder of being alive, reminding us of the profound interconnectedness and interdependence of all things.

Probability, rooted in the principles of statistics and mathematical analysis, offers a framework for understanding the likelihood of events occurring based on empirical data and observed patterns. From coin tosses to card games, probability provides a tool for quantifying the likelihood of various outcomes and making informed decisions in uncertain situations. While probability offers a valuable tool for predicting and understanding the likelihood of events in a deterministic universe, it falls short in capturing the full complexity and richness of synchronicity. Unlike probability, which operates within the confines of linear causality and predictable outcomes, synchronicity transcends traditional notions of cause and effect, encompassing the mysterious interplay of meaning, significance, and interconnectedness that underlies the fabric of reality. In this sense, synchronicity invites us to reimagine reality not as a fixed and deterministic system governed by probabilistic laws, but as a dynamic and interconnected web of possibilities where the boundaries between past, present, and future blur, and the unimaginable becomes possible.

By embracing the enigmatic nature of synchronicity and its potential to transform our understanding of reality, we embark on a journey of exploration and discovery, venturing into the uncharted territories of consciousness, creativity, and the human spirit. Healing synchronicities often involve a process of inner transformation and self-discovery, as individuals confront and release old patterns, traumas, or limitations that are inhibiting their health and well-being. By listening to the messages encoded within their bodies and emotions, individuals can unlock the healing power that lies dormant within them, reclaiming their vitality, wholeness, and resilience to face life's challenges with courage and grace. This process of inner healing and self-discovery is not always easy and may require individuals to confront their deepest fears, insecurities, and wounds. By embracing the healing journey with courage and compassion, individuals can tap into their innate capacity for resilience and transformation, reclaiming their power and agency in the process. Healing synchronicities offer opportunities for individuals to reconnect with their authentic selves, aligning with their true purpose and potential in life. As they release the burdens of the past and embrace the possibilities of the present moment, individuals can experience profound shifts in consciousness and well-being, leading to greater vitality, joy, and fulfillment in all areas of their lives. Ultimately, healing synchronicities remind us that the journey of healing is not just about overcoming illness or injury, but about reclaiming our wholeness and embracing the fullness of our being.

At its essence, synchronicity reveals the interconnectedness of all things, illustrating that nothing happens in isolation. Rather than viewing the world as a series of random occurrences, synchronicity urges us to recognize the underlying harmony that permeates every aspect of our lives. It is a testament to the intelligence and creativity inherent in the universe, guiding us along paths we may not have dared to tread otherwise.

Embracing synchronicity opens doors to new possibilities and insights, enriching our journey through life. By fostering an attitude of openness and trust, we invite synchronicity to illuminate our path, guiding us toward growth and transformation. It is a reminder that there is a deeper order at play, even amidst the chaos of our everyday experiences.

While probability offers a framework for understanding the likelihood of events based on empirical data, synchronicity transcends such deterministic notions. Unlike probability, which operates within the confines of cause and effect, synchronicity encompasses a realm where meaning and significance intertwine in ways that defy rational explanation. It beckons us to venture beyond the boundaries of our understanding, into a realm where the unimaginable becomes possible.

Synchronicity often manifests as healing, catalyzing inner transformation and self-discovery. As we confront old patterns and traumas, synchronicity offers a guiding light, illuminating the path toward wholeness and resilience. It is a journey of courage and compassion, as we navigate the depths of our being, reclaiming our power and agency along the way.

Healing synchronicities remind us that the journey toward wholeness is not merely about overcoming illness or injury. It is a profound process of self-realization, aligning with our true purpose and potential in life. As we release the burdens of the past and embrace the present moment, we unlock the fullness of our being, experiencing greater vitality, joy, and fulfillment.

In essence, synchronicity invites us to embrace the mystery and wonder of the universe. It is a reminder that there is more to life than meets the eye, and that the unseen forces guiding our journey are filled with infinite wisdom and possibility. As we surrender to the flow of synchronicity, we embark on a journey of exploration and discovery, forever transformed by the magic that surrounds us.

Synchronicity, often regarded as a phenomenon that transcends conventional explanations, continues to captivate and intrigue individuals across various walks of life. Its enigmatic nature defies easy categorization, challenging our understanding of reality and urging us to delve deeper into the mysteries of existence.

One of the most remarkable aspects of synchronicity is its ability to reveal the hidden patterns and connections that underlie the fabric of reality. Through synchronistic events, seemingly unrelated occurrences are woven together, forming a rich tapestry of meaning and significance. These moments of serendipity serve as gentle reminders that the universe is far more interconnected than we often perceive, inviting us to contemplate the deeper truths that lie beyond the surface of our everyday experiences.

Synchronicity serves as a catalyst for personal growth and transformation. By inviting us to embrace the unknown and relinquish our need for control, synchronistic events push us out of our comfort zones and into uncharted territory. In doing so, they provide fertile ground for self-discovery. The exploration of synchronicity extends beyond individual experiences and into the collective consciousness of humanity. Across cultures and civilizations, there are countless tales of synchronistic events that have shaped the course of history and influenced the trajectory of entire societies. From ancient myths and legends to modern-day anecdotes, these stories serve as a testament to the enduring power of synchronicity to unite us in shared purpose and destiny.

In the realm of relationships, synchronicity often plays a pivotal role in bringing people together and forging deep connections that transcend time and space. Whether it be the serendipitous encounter of soulmates or the timely assistance of kindred spirits, synchronistic bonds serve as reminders of the interconnected web of relationships that sustains us all. Through these meaningful connections, we come to recognize that we are not alone in our journey but are instead part of a larger tapestry of love and support that spans the cosmos.

Furthermore, the study of synchronicity holds great promise for expanding our understanding of the nature of reality itself. While traditional scientific methods may struggle to account for the seemingly irrational nature of synchronistic events, there is growing recognition within the scientific community of the need to embrace a more holistic and inclusive approach to knowledge. By integrating insights from fields such as quantum physics, psychology, and consciousness studies, researchers are beginning to unravel the underlying mechanisms that govern synchronicity and its profound implications for our understanding of the universe.

In the realm of spirituality and mysticism, synchronicity is often seen as a manifestation of the divine intelligence that animates all of creation. From the perspective of spiritual traditions around the world, synchronistic events are viewed as sacred messages from the universe, guiding us along our spiritual path and reminding us of our interconnectedness with all of life. Whether through dreams, visions, or spontaneous insights, these synchronistic experiences serve as portals to higher states of consciousness and spiritual awakening.

The practice of cultivating mindfulness and presence can serve as a powerful catalyst for recognizing and embracing synchronicity in our lives. By quieting the incessant chatter of the mind and attuning ourselves to the subtle rhythms of the universe, we create space for synchronistic events to unfold naturally and effortlessly. Through practices such as meditation, yoga, and deep listening, we can cultivate a state of receptivity and openness that allows us to more fully participate in the dance of synchronicity.

In essence, synchronicity is a profound reminder of the interconnectedness and interdependence of all things in the grand tapestry of existence. It challenges us to transcend the limitations of our rational minds and embrace the mysteries of the universe with childlike wonder and curiosity. As we open ourselves to the transformative power of synchronicity, we discover a world filled with infinite possibilities and potentials, where the miraculous becomes the norm and the ordinary becomes extraordinary, encouraging us to explore new facets of ourselves and uncover hidden potentials that may have remained dormant otherwise.

In the realm of creativity and innovation, synchronicity plays a profound role in inspiring breakthroughs and paradigm shifts. Countless artists, scientists, and visionaries throughout history have attributed their most significant discoveries to moments of synchronicity, where seemingly unrelated ideas or insights converge in unexpected ways. These creative leaps serve as a testament to the inherent intelligence of the universe, which constantly seeks to express itself through the myriad forms of human expression.

Furthermore, the experience of synchronicity often evokes a sense of awe and wonder, reminding us of the profound mystery that permeates all of existence. Whether it manifests as a chance encounter with a long-lost friend or a series of uncanny coincidences that defy explanation, synchronicity invites us to pause and marvel at the intricate dance of life unfolding around us. In these moments of synchronistic grace, we catch glimpses of a reality far more expansive and magical than we had previously imagined.

At its core, synchronicity is a deeply transformative force that invites us to embrace the fullness of our being. By surrendering to the flow of synchronistic events and allowing ourselves to be guided by the wisdom of the universe, we open ourselves to a world of infinite possibilities and potentials. In doing so, we embark on a journey of self-discovery and evolution, where each synchronistic encounter serves as a stepping stone on the path toward greater understanding and enlightenment.

Synchronicity remains a profound and ineffable mystery that continues to intrigue and inspire seekers of truth and wisdom around the world. As we navigate the complexities of existence, let us remain open to the synchronistic signs and signals that guide our journey, trusting in the inherent intelligence of the universe to lead us toward our highest destiny. For in the dance of synchronicity, we discover not only the interconnectedness of all things but also the boundless potential that resides within each and every one of us.

The recognition and integration of synchronicity into our daily lives can lead to profound shifts in perception and behavior. By acknowledging the interconnectedness of all things and embracing the synchronistic flow of life, we cultivate a deeper sense of trust and surrender to the unfolding of events. Instead of resisting or trying to control the outcomes, we learn to navigate with grace and ease, knowing that we are guided by a wisdom far greater than our own.

In the realm of personal growth and development, synchronicity serves as a powerful mirror reflecting back to us the patterns and beliefs that shape our reality. Through synchronistic events, we are often confronted with opportunities for healing and transformation, inviting us to release old wounds and limitations that no longer serve us. By embracing these moments of synchronicity with openness and courage, we can catalyze profound shifts in consciousness and move towards greater levels of authenticity and wholeness.

Furthermore, the recognition of synchronicity can serve as a source of inspiration and guidance in times of uncertainty or adversity. When faced with challenges or dilemmas, we can turn to the synchronistic signs and symbols that appear in our lives for direction and clarity. Whether it be a chance encounter with a wise mentor or a series of meaningful coincidences that point us in a new direction, synchronicity offers a guiding light amidst the darkness, illuminating the path forward with hope and possibility.

In the realm of creativity and innovation, synchronicity acts as a catalyst for breakthroughs and discoveries that transcend the boundaries of conventional thinking. By opening ourselves to the synchronistic flow of inspiration and insight, we tap into a wellspring of creativity that lies beyond the confines of the rational mind. Whether it be in the realms of art, science, or entrepreneurship, synchronicity empowers us to think outside the box and pioneer new frontiers of possibility.

The cultivation of synchronicity can lead to greater harmony and balance in our relationships and interactions with others. By recognizing the interconnectedness of all beings and honoring the sacredness of every encounter, we foster a sense of compassion and empathy that transcends personal boundaries. In doing so, we create space for meaningful connections to flourish, grounded in a deep sense of mutual respect and understanding.

The recognition and integration of synchronicity into our lives hold the potential to transform our experience of reality in profound and meaningful ways. By embracing the interconnectedness of all things and surrendering to the synchronistic flow of life, we open ourselves to a world of infinite possibility and potential. As we cultivate a deeper sense of trust and receptivity, we discover that synchronicity is not merely a random occurrence but a guiding principle that illuminates our path and empowers us to live with purpose, passion, and joy.

References

"Synchronicity: An Acausal Connecting Principle" by Carl Jung
Publisher: Princeton University Press
Year: 1973

"The Roots of Coincidence" by Arthur Koestler
Publisher: Vintage
Year: 1972

"The Secret Language of Synchronicity: Deciphering the Words & Wisdom of Meaningful Coincidence" by Trish & Rob MacGregor
Publisher: Career Press
Year: 2011

"Coincidence: A Matter of Chance - or Synchronicity?" by Brian Inglis
Publisher: Arrow Books
Year: 1990

"The Power of Coincidence: How Life Shows Us What We Need to Know" by David Richo
Publisher: Shambhala
Year: 2007

"Synchronicity: Empower Your Life with the Gift of Coincidence" by Chris Mackey
Publisher: Hierophant Publishing
Year: 2015

"Synchronicity: The Bridge Between Matter and Mind" by F. David Peat
Publisher: Bantam
Year: 1987

"The Tao of Jung: The Way of Integrity" by David H. Rosen
Publisher: Viking
Year: 1997

"The Synchronicity War: Part 1" by Dietmar Wehr
Publisher: CreateSpace Independent Publishing Platform
Year: 2013

"Coincidence Studies: Rationality, Irrationality, and the Absurd" by Stanley A. Plotkin
Publisher: University Press of America
Year: 1993

"Signs: The Secret Language of the Universe" by Laura Lynne Jackson
Publisher: Spiegel & Grau
Year: 2019

"The Seven Secrets of Synchronicity: Your Guide to Finding Meaning in Signs Big and Small" by Trish MacGregor
Publisher: Adams Media
Year: 2011

"Synchronicity, Science, and Soul-Making: Understanding Jungian Synchronicity Through Physics, Buddhism, and Philosophy" by Victor Mansfield
Publisher: Open Court
Year: 1995

"Synchronicity: The Art of Coincidence, Choice, and Unlocking Your Mind" by Kirby Surprise
Publisher: Inner Traditions
Year: 2012

"Coincidence and Counterfactuality: Plotting Time and Space in Narrative Fiction" by Hilary P. Dannenberg
Publisher: Cambridge University Press
Year: 2008

"The Tapestry of Reality: The Quest for Meaning in the 21st Century" by K. Victor Ujor
Publisher: CreateSpace Independent Publishing Platform
Year: 2018

"The Power of Coincidence: Discover the Science of Luck and Spontaneous Manifestation" by David Rich
Publisher: Watkins Publishing
Year: 2011

"The God Hypothesis: Extraterrestrial Life and Its Implications for Science and Religion" by Joe Lewels
Publisher: Inner Traditions
Year: 2010

"Cosmic Coincidences: Dark Matter, Mankind, and Anthropic Cosmology" by R.H. Sanders
Publisher: Pegasus Publishing
Year: 2002

"The Celestine Prophecy: An Adventure" by James Redfield
Publisher: Warner Books
Year: 1993

"Synchronicity: Nature and Psyche in an Interconnected Universe" by Joseph Cambray
Publisher: Texas A&M University Press
Year: 2009

"Psychology of the Future: Lessons from Modern Consciousness Research" by Stanislav Grof
Publisher: State University of New York Press
Year: 2000

"The Web of Life: A New Scientific Understanding of Living Systems" by Fritjof Capra
Publisher: Anchor
Year: 1996

"The Holographic Universe" by Michael Talbot
Publisher: Harper Perennial
Year: 1991

"The Cosmic Serpent: DNA and the Origins of Knowledge" by Jeremy Narby
Publisher: TarcherPerigee
Year: 1999

"Coincidences: Touched by Divine or Random Acts of Nature?" by Joseph Mazur
Publisher: Scribner
Year: 2017

"Synchronicity: Science, Myth, and the Trickster" by Allan Combs
Publisher: Paragon House
Year: 2002

"The Source Field Investigations: The Hidden Science and Lost Civilizations Behind the 2012 Prophecies" by David Wilcock
Publisher: Dutton
Year: 2011

"The Fourth Turning: An American Prophecy" by William Strauss and Neil Howe
Publisher: Broadway Books
Year: 1997

"Synchrodestiny: Harnessing the Infinite Power of Coincidence to Create Miracles" by Deepak Chopra
Publisher: Harmony
Year: 2003

"The Fabric of Reality: The Science of Parallel Universes and Its Implications" by David Deutsch
Publisher: Penguin Books
Year: 1998

"Beyond Coincidence: One Man's Experiences with Psychic Phenomena" by Stan Kelsey
Publisher: Starfire Publishing
Year: 2015

"The Hidden Messages in Water" by Masaru Emoto
Publisher: Atria Books
Year: 2004

"The Power of Now: A Guide to Spiritual Enlightenment" by Eckhart Tolle
Publisher: New World Library
Year: 1997

"The Art of Coincidence: Transforming Coincidences into a Life of Grace" by Meg Lundstrom
Publisher: Atria Books/Beyond Words
Year: 2007

"The Source: The Secrets of the Universe, the Science of the Brain" by Tara Swart

Publisher: HarperOne
Year: 2019

"The Field: The Quest for the Secret Force of the Universe"
by Lynne McTaggart
Publisher: Harper Perennial
Year: 2008

"The Hidden Reality: Parallel Universes and the Deep
Laws of the Cosmos" by Brian Greene
Publisher: Vintage Books
Year: 2012

"Do You QuantumThink?: New Thinking That Will Rock
Your World" by Dianne Collins
Publisher: SelectBooks
Year: 2011

"The Intention Experiment: Using Your Thoughts to
Change Your Life and the World" by Lynne McTaggart
Publisher: Free Press
Year: 2007

This list encompasses a wide range of perspectives on
synchronicity, coincidence, and related topics, providing
readers with various insights and interpretations.

Index

www.ingramcontent.com/pod-product-compliance
Lightning Source LLC
Chambersburg PA
CBHW071929150726
47999CB00001B/156